David
Pla

The Changing Room, Cromwell, Life Class

The Changing Room: 'It's about exactly what it is: Storey offers us, with an unforced tenderness, the shifting moods of everyday experience ... the scene is busy, purposeful and exhilarating. You'd never imagine realism could be this theatrical ... *The Changing Room* takes you into its world in a way few plays achieve.' *Independent on Sunday*

'An excellent example of Storey's ability to evoke lives from snippets and a society from those lives. Less becomes more. He calls the play *The Changing Room* and leaves you feeling that you are seeing a changing world.' *The Times*

Cromwell: 'An exploration of the vices and virtues of the English Puritan instinct using the historical associations of the Cromwellian period. On top of that it is also an impressive piece of poetic drama employing a spare, flinty, concrete language that seems to be hewn out of rock ... Storey manages to make the work both specific and allusive ... its primal conflicts between principle and expediency, the individual and the community are perennially relevant ... a rich and complex play.' *Guardian*

Life Class: 'I have just had in the theatre an experience so remarkable that I doubt if I shall ever forget it ... its portrait of a man, dangerous, controlled, and wounded, who brings down his whole career in one enormous gesture signifying that all we hold of good from the past is now incapable of renewal and irrelevant to our present needs ... *Life Class* is not merely a very good play. It is a blazing masterpiece ... It is a tremendous experience and its glare lights up the sky.' *Sunday Times*

David Storey: unique in his generation of writers, David Storey's achievements are divided equally between his work as as novelist and as a playwright. Born in 1933, the son of a mineworker, he went to the Slade School of Fine Art in London and had various jobs, ranging from farm labouring and showground tent-erecting to professional rugby league football and schoolteaching. Among his novels are *This Sporting Life*, which won the Macmillan Fiction Award in 1960 and was filmed, *Flight Into Camden*, which won the John Llewelyn Rhys Memorial Prize, and *Radcliffe*, which won the Somerset Maugham Award in 1963. Later novels include *Pasmore*, a Booker finalist and winner of the Faber Memorial Prize, *Saville*, winner of the Booker Prize in 1976, and most recently, *A Serious Man*. His plays include *The Contractor, Home* and *The Changing Room* – each of which won the New York Critics Best Play of the Year Award – *In Celebration*, which was filmed, *Life Class* and *The Farm*: all of these plays were premièred at the Royal Court Theatre; his two later plays, *Early Days* and *The March on Russia*, were presented at the National Theatre in the 1980s. *Stages* was premièred at the Royal National Theatre in 1992. David Storey lives in London. He was married in 1956 and has four children.

DAVID STOREY

Plays: 3

**The Changing Room
Cromwell
Life Class**

with an introduction by the author

Methuen Drama

METHUEN CONTEMPORARY DRAMATISTS

This collection first published in Great Britain 1998
by Methuen Drama
Random House, 20 Vauxhall Bridge Road, London SW1V 2SA
and Australia, New Zealand and South Africa

The Changing Room first published in Great Britain in 1972 by Jonathan
Cape Ltd; 1996 in the Royal Court Writers Series by Methuen Drama
Copyright © 1972, 1996 by David Storey
Cromwell first published in Great Britain in 1973 by Jonathan Cape Ltd
Copyright © 1973 by David Storey
Life Class first published in Great Britain in 1975 by Jonathan Cape Ltd
Copyright © 1975 by David Storey

Introduction and this collection copyright © 1998 by David Storey

The author has asserted his moral rights

ISBN 0–413–72350–X

Random House UK Limited Reg. No. 954009

A CIP catalogue record for this book
is available from the British Library

Typeset by Deltatype Ltd, Birkenhead, Merseyside
Printed and bound in Great Britain by
Cox & Wyman, Reading, Berkshire

Contents

A Chronology
of plays, novels and poetry

Introduction

One Saturday night, some time in 1970, I was standing at the back of the stalls in the Fortune Theatre, London, watching a production of *The Contractor*, transferred there from a production the previous year at the Royal Court. Earlier I had been talking with the actors in the (then) dilapidated Green Room, they filling in time between the matinée and evening performances: now I watched them enter the stage and – a full house – transform themselves from the individuals I'd earlier been talking to, to the characters of the play. This curious transformation from private to public personae – and back again – I'd been conscious of before but something on this occasion struck me anew: the essence, or nature of the act itself: it occurred in a room (the stage) which was itself transformed by the actors' arrival – and departure. Why not, I reflected, write a play called 'The Green Room' – and, indeed, once I'd settled down to the idea, at home, I did; at least, I began – swiftly to conclude it had, in one form or another, been done before: backstage, or offstage dramas had had a number of significant and successful precedents.

At the time of witnessing this transformation process, however, it had also struck me that the activity I was observing was not unlike that associated with any performance – not least, since I had at one time played rugby league football, that of a professional footballer: *he* came into a room, changed from a private individual (conspicuously) into a public performer (he wore a uniform), went out, performed, returned, reverted to his previous persona – and departed: simultaneously the room itself underwent a not dissimilar transformation: empty to begin with, gradually filling, emptying again, the room, in short, both object and subject, active and passive: it changed those within it and, in turn, was changed itself. This magical process seemed, on reflection, a legacy from my earlier theatrical experience (*Home*, with Gielgud and Richardson, was concurrently running in the West End).

The play owed much in production to my collaboration (three plays, one feature film) with Lindsay Anderson: casting was demanding and thorough: actors who were physically suitable were not necessarily suitable temperamentally: matching temperament to physique, in fact, took a very long time (over six hundred actors were finally auditioned, painstakingly dragooned by Gillian Diamond, the casting director at the Court: a final, desperate resort was to advertise in the London *Evening Standard*). Many of the cast, subsequently, went on to substantial actorial careers: Alun Armstrong, Michael Elphick, Brian Glover, Warren Clarke, Mark McManus, Edward Peel, David Daker amongst them, while John Barrett, John Rae, Paul Dawkins and Edward Judd added weight and experience (and subtlety) to what might otherwise have been described as a starkly idiosyncratic text.

First produced at the Royal Court in 1971, it transferred to the Globe Theatre where, after a highly successful introduction, it was killed off by the 1972 miners' strike – ironically, because my father had been a miner – and, to the extent that anyone could in London, I supported the aspirations of the strike itself.

Restitution of a sort was achieved in New York where a vivid production of the play by Michael Rudman, mounted with American actors, transferred from the Long Wharf Theatre, New Haven, to Broadway where it ran for the better part of a year and won the principal annual play award. Since then it has been produced in countries as diverse as Hungary, Argentina, France, Italy and Japan, and was revived by the English Stage Company at the Duke of York's Theatre for their Royal Court Classics Season in 1996.

Cromwell was written when the war in Vietnam, and the troubles in Northern Ireland, were at their height. It began with an idea carried on from *The Changing Room* – namely, a group of actors meeting to rehearse a play (a similar transformation from private to public worlds envisaged). Within two or three pages of starting the play, however, I noticed that the text to be rehearsed had already taken over the play itself – an allegory (the play within the play) and, perhaps as a consequence of that, 'poetic' in style. Helplessness at what was happening elsewhere (remorseless killing) infused the writing, turning what was intended into something else.

It was produced at the Royal Court in 1973, directed by Anthony Page (a unique combination of enthusiasm and patience) and, like *The Changing Room*, was evocatively designed by Jocelyn Herbert. Brian Cox played the principal role of the recruit turned pacifist, and Albert Finney a subordinate role of an itinerant Irish labourer. To some extent an enigma, the play's form emerged at a time when I was much enthralled by naturalistic – or poeticised naturalistic writing, a sudden transposition to something approaching free verse reflecting, to a degree, the dilemma explicit in the play itself: how to reconcile humanity's insatiable appetite for destruction with a longing for transcendence and peace.

In a curious way, this play and *The Changing Room* were implicit in the formation of the third in this volume, *Life Class*: that too had its source in that Saturday night experience at the back of the Fortune Theatre: watching *The Contractor* from *behind* the heads of the audience I was struck by the nature of an event in which the viewer views the viewer viewing the object (performance art, at the time, very much to the fore).

Allott (a lot: everything: a munificence) is an art teacher in a northern provincial art school (I had attended one such, at Wakefield, in my late teens). Conceived as something not unakin to an existential Prospero, he creates, as if with the audience's participation, a class, or 'event' – in his designation, an 'invisible event' since the participants are not consciously aware of their involvement. The materials of this event (or performance: his self-declared 'work of art') are, as for most artists, those of his daily existence: in this instance, a group of (largely) unsympathtic (and conceivably ungifted) youths who, for one reason or another – fortuity – have found their way into what might

be described as his allegorised arena (i.e., onto his 'canvas')
– a phenomenological act, and perception, which, Allott
concludes, is, like all 'art', expressive – an embodiment – of
his time.

This (difficult) play was again miraculously directed by
Lindsay Anderson and felicitously designed by Jocelyn
Herbert, and again had the benefit of meticulous casting –
together with the central presence of Alan Bates who
balanced the mercurial, if not the inexpressible, on the
edge, the very rarified edge, of his sensitised performance.

The play transferred from the Court to the Duke of
York's where its elliptical nature probably confounded as
many as it seduced by its inner agenda.

The idea of transformation, therefore, lies as a theme
behind all three plays, an aspiration to explore – ideally, to
define – the moment when the actual (i.e., what is
happening now) moves beyond itself into what might be
described as reality: that which includes actuality and
everything beyond it: numinosity, it might be described, or
immanence, the essence, approached through ritual, of
religion as well as art.

David Storey, 1998

The Changing Room

To Jake

Characters

Harry, *cleaner, 50–60*
Patsy, *wing threequarter, 23–5*
Fielding, *forward, 35–6*
Mic Morley, *forward, 28*
Kendal, *forward, 29*
Luke, *masseur, 40–50*
Fenchurch, *wing threequarter, 23–5*
Colin Jagger, *centre threequarter, 26*
Trevor, *full-back, 26*
Walsh, *forward, 35–40*
Sandford, *assistant trainer, 40*
Barry Copley, *scrum-half, 27–8*
Jack Stringer, *centre threequarter, 30*
Bryan Atkinson, *forward, 32*
Billy Spencer, *reserve, 20*
John Clegg, *hooker, 30*
Frank Moore, *reserve, 21*
Danny Crosby, *trainer, 45–50*
Cliff Owens, *stand-off half, 30–32*
Tallon, *referee*
Thornton, *chairman, 50*
Mackendrick, *club secretary, 60*

The Changing Room was first presented at the Royal Court Theatre, London, on 9 November 1971, with the following cast:

Harry	John Barrett
Patsy	Jim Norton
Fielding	David Daker
Mic Morley	Edward Peel
Kendal	Warren Clarke
Luke	Don McKillop
Fenchurch	Peter Childs
Colin Jagger	Mark McManus
Trevor	Michael Elphick
Walsh	Edward Judd
Sandford	Brian Glover
Barry Copley	Geoffrey Hinsliff
Jack Stringer	David Hill
Bryan Atkinson	Peter Schofield
Billy Spencer	Alun Armstrong
John Clegg	Matthew Guinness
Frank Moore	John Price
Danny Crosby	Barry Keegan
Cliff Owens	Frank Mills
Tallon	Brian Lawson
Thornton	Paul Dawkins
Mackendrick	John Rae

Directed by Lindsay Anderson
Designed by Jocelyn Herbert

The Changing Room was produced in the Royal Court Classics Season at the Duke of York's Theatre, London, on 1 February 1996, with the following cast:

Harry	Ewan Hooper
Patsy	Chris Gascoyne
Fielding	Chris Walker
Mic Morley	Jonathan Magnanti
Kendal	Brendan Coyle
Luke	Paul Rider
Fenchurch	Tim Dantay
Colin Jagger	Louis Hilyer
Trevor	David Michaels
Walsh	Philip Whitchurch
Sandford	Philip Martin Brown
Barry Copley	David MacCreedy
Jack Stringer	Simon Wolfe
Bryan Atkinson	Roger Morlidge
Billy Spencer	Andrew Cryer
John Clegg	Stephen Bent
Frank Moore	Jason Pitt
Danny Crosby	Simon Rouse
Cliff Owens	Nicholas McGaughey
Tallon	Roy North
Thornton	David Hargreaves
Mackendrick	Alex McAvoy

Directed by James Macdonald
Designed by Hildegard Bechtler

Act One

A changing room; afternoon. The light comes from glazed panels high in the wall and from an electric light.

Across the back of the stage is the main changing bench, set up against the wall and running its entire length. A set of hooks, one for each player, is fastened at head height to the wall, with the name of a player above each hook. Underneath the bench, below each hook, is a locker, also labelled. A jersey and a pair of shorts have been set out beneath one of the hooks. A rubbing-down table with an adjustable head-rest stands in front of the bench. Stage right, a glazed door opens to an entrance porch. Downstage left is a fireplace, with a bucket of coal, overhung by a mirror advertising ale. Upstage left is the open entry to the bath and showers: buckets, stool, hose and tap, etc. Downstage right is a wooden door, closed, leading to the offices. A second table stands against the wall. There's a pair of metal scales with individual metal weights on a metal arm. By the rubbing-down table stands a large wickerwork basket. A wooden chair with a rounded back is set against the wall, stage left.

Tannoy music is being played, light, militaristic.

Harry *enters from the bath. He's a broken-down man, small, stooped, in shirt-sleeves, rolled, and a sleeveless pullover. He's smoking and carries a sweeping-brush, on the lookout for anything he might have missed. He sweeps, looks round the floor, sweeps; finally lifts corner of the boxed-in rubbing-down table and sweeps the debris underneath. Takes out his cigarette, looks round, finds nowhere to drop it, then crosses to the fire; drops it in, sets the brush against the wall, puts coal from the bucket on the fire, warms his hands, shivers.*

Patsy *enters from the porch. He's a smart, lightly built man, very well groomed, hair greased, collar of an expensive overcoat turned up. Brisk, businesslike, narcissistic, no evident sense of humour.*

Patsy   Harry . . .

Harry   Patsy . . .

Patsy   Cold.

Harry   Bloody freezing, lad. (*Rubs his hands; reaches to the fire again.*)

Patsy, *evidently familiar with his routine, goes to his locker. Gets out his boots, unfolds his jersey and shorts already lying on the bench.*

Patsy   No towel.

Harry   No. No. Just fetching those . . . (*Takes his brush and exits through bath entrance.*)

Patsy, *having checked his jersey, examined its number (2), collar, etc. – no marks – does the same with his boots: laces, studs, lining. He then crosses to the fire, takes out a comb from an inside pocket and smooths his hair down in the mirror. He's doing this as* **Harry** *re-enters carrying several neatly folded towels. He puts one on the bench by* **Patsy**'s *peg, then goes to the wickerwork basket, lifts the lid and gets out several more towels. Having checked them, counting soundlessly to himself, he puts them all in the basket, save three which he begins to arrange on the massage table.*

Patsy, *having combed his hair and admired himself in the mirror, clears his nose and spits in the fire.*

Harry (*laying out towels*)   Thought it'd be snowed off.

Patsy   Snow?

Harry   Bloody forecast.

Patsy   Not cancel ought in this dump, I can tell you . . . Shoulder . . . I've no skin on from here to here. There's not a blade o' grass on that bloody pitch . . . sithee . . . look at that . . .

Pulls up his sleeve. **Harry** *looks across with no evident interest.*

Harry   Aye.

Patsy   Watered t'bloody pitch we 'ad last week. Froze over ten minutes after. Took a run at t'bloody ball . . . took off . . . must have travelled twenty bloody yards without having lift a finger.

Harry   Aye.

Patsy   Ice.

Harry *is laying out the rest of the jerseys now, and shorts.*

Patsy Be better off with a pair of skates. (*Glances behind him, into the mirror; smooths hair.*) If there's a young woman comes asking for me afterwards, will you tell her to wait up in the office? Be frozen to death out theer.

Harry Aye . . .

Patsy By Christ . . . (*Rubs his hands, standing with his back to the fire.*)

Harry Comes from Russia.

Patsy What?

Harry Cold . . . Comes fro' Russia . . .

Patsy Oh . . . (*Nods.*)

Harry Read a book . . . they had a special machine . . . blew these winds o'er, you see . . . specially freezing . . . mixed it with a chemical . . . frozen ought . . . Froze the entire country . . . Then Ireland . . . Then crossed over to America and froze it out . . . Then, when everything wa' frozen, they came o'er in special boots and took over . . . Here . . . America . . . Nobody twigged it. Nobody cottoned on, you see.

Patsy Oh . . . (*Glances at himself in mirror again.*) You think that's what's happening now, then?

Harry Cold enough . . . Get no warning . . . Afore you know what's happening . . . Ruskies here.

Patsy Couldn't be worse than this lot.

Harry What?

Patsy Stopped ten quid i' bloody tax last week . . . I tell you . . . I'm paying t'government to keep me i' bloody work . . . madhouse . . . If I had my time o'er again I'd emigrate . . . America . . . Australia . . .

Harry Wherever you go they'll find you out.

Patsy What?

Harry   Ruskies . . . Keep your name down in a bloody book . . . (*Looks across.*) Won't make any difference if you've voted socialist. Have you down theer . . . up against a wall . . .

Patsy   Thy wants to read one or two bloody facts, old lad.

Harry   Facts? What facts? . . . I read in one paper that in twenty-five years not one country on earth'll not be communist . . .

Patsy *crosses back to his peg and starts taking off his overcoat.*

Don't worry. There'll be no lakin' bloody football then.

Patsy   They lake football i' Russia as much as they lake it here.

Harry   Aye . . .

Harry *waits, threatening;* **Patsy** *doesn't answer, preoccupied with his overcoat.*

You: football . . . You: coalmine . . . You: factory . . . You: air force . . . You . . . *Siberia.*

Patsy   Haven't you got a bloody coathanger? Damn well ask for one each week.

Harry   Aye. Don't worry . . . (*Starts to go.*) Not bloody listen until they find it's bloody well too late. (*Goes off to the bath entrance, disgruntled.*)

Fielding *enters: large, well-built man, slow, easy-going, thirty-five to thirty-six. He's dressed in an overcoat and muffler; he has a strip of plaster above his left eye.*

Fielding   Patsy.

Patsy   Fieldy . . .

Fielding   Freeze your knuckles off today. (*Blows in hands, goes over to fire; stoops, warms hands.*) By Christ . . .

Patsy *is holding up his coat in one hand, dusting it down lightly, paying no attention to* **Fielding**'s *entrance.*

Harry *comes back in with wooden coathanger.*

Harry   Have no bloody servants theer, you know.

Patsy (*examining coat*)   What's that?

Harry   No servants. Do your own bloody carrying theer.

Gives **Patsy** *the hanger and goes back to laying out the playing-kit.*

Fielding   What's that, Harry? (*Winks to* **Patsy**.)

Patsy   Bloody Russians. Going to be invaded.

Harry   Don't you worry. It can happen any time, you know.

Patsy   Going to freeze us, with a special liquid . . . Then come over . . . (*To* **Harry**.) What wa're it? . . . i' special boots.

Harry   It all goes back, you know.

Patsy   Back?

Harry   To bloody Moscow . . . Ought you say here's reported back . . . Keep all thy names in a special book.

Fielding   Keep thy name in a special bloody book . . . Riley . . . First name: Harry . . . Special qualifications: can talk out of the back of his bloody head.

Harry   Don't you worry.

Fielding   Nay, I'm not worried. They can come here any day of the bloody week for me. Sup of ale . . .

Patsy   Ten fags . . .

Fielding   That's all I need. (*Sneezes hugely. Shakes his head, gets out his handkerchief, blows his nose, lengthily and noisily.*) Come on, then, Harry . . . Switch it off.

After gazing at **Fielding**, *threatening,* **Harry** *turns off the Tannoy.*

I thought o' ringing up this morning . . . Looked out o' the bloody winder. Frost . . . (*Crosses over to* **Patsy**.) Got this

house, now, just outside the town . . . wife's idea, not mine
. . . bloody fields . . . hardly a bloody sign of human life . . .
cows . . . half a dozen sheep . . . goats . . .

Starts peeling the plaster from above his eye. **Patsy** *pays no attention,
arranging his coat on the hanger and picking off one or two bits.*

Middle of bloody nowhere . . . if I can't see a wall outside on
t'window I don't feel as though I'm living in a house . . .
How's it look?

Patsy (*glances up, briefly*)   All right.

Fielding   Bloody fist. Loose forra'd . . . Copped him one
afore the end. Had a leg like a bloody melon . . . (*Feeling the
cut.*) Get Lukey to put on a bit of grease . . . Should be all
right. How's your shoulder?

Patsy   All right. (*Eases it.*) Came in early. Get it strapped.
(*Indicates, however, that there's no one here.*)

Fielding   Where we lived afore, you know, everything you
could bloody want: pit, boozer, bloody dogs. As for now . . .
trees, hedges, miles o' bloody grass . . . (*Inspecting his kit which
Harry has now hung up.*) Weer's the jock-straps, Harry? . . . I
thought of ringing up and backing out. Flu . . . some such
like. (*Sneezes.*) By God . . . He'll have me lakin' here, will
Harry, wi' me bloody cobblers hanging out.

Morley *has now entered from the porch: thick-set, squat figure, dark-
haired. Wears a jacket, unbuttoned, with a sweater underneath; hard,
rough, uncomplicated figure.*

Nah, Morley, lad, then: how's thy keeping?

Morley   Shan't be a second . . . Just o'd on. (*Goes straight
over to the bath entrance, unbuttoning his flies.*)

He's followed in by **Kendal**: *tall, rather well-built, late twenties,
wearing an old overcoat with a scarf, and carrying a paper parcel. A
worn, somewhat faded man.*

Harry *has gone to the basket and is now getting out a pile of jock-
straps which he lays on the table.*

Kendal (*to* **Harry**)   Here . . . see about my boots? Bloody stud missing last Thursday . . . (*To* **Fielding**.) Supposed to check them every bloody week. Come up to training and nearly bust me bloody ankle. God Christ, they don't give a sod about bloody ought up here . . . Patsy . . .

Patsy   Kenny . . . (*Having hung up his coat, starts taking off his jacket.*)

Kendal (*to* **Fielding**)   Bought one of these electric tool-sets . . .

Fielding (*to* **Patsy**)   Tool-sets . . .

Patsy *nods.*

Fielding   Got all the tools that I need, Kenny.

Kendal   Bloody saw . . . drill, bloody polisher. Just look.

Fielding   What do you do with that? (*Picks out a tool.*)

Kendal   Dunno.

Patsy   Takes stones out of hosses' hoofs, more like.

They laugh.

Morley *comes back in.*

Fielding   Dirty bugger. Pisses i' the bloody bath.

Morley   Been in that bog, then, have you? (*To* **Harry**.) You want to clean it out.

Harry   That lavatory was new this season . . . (*Indicating* **Fielding**.) He'll tell you. One we had afore I wouldn't have used.

Morley *goes straight to the business of getting changed: coat off, sweater, then shoes and socks; then starts examining his ankle.*

Fielding   Harry doesn't use a lavatory, do you?

Morley   Piles it up behind the bloody posts.

Fielding   Dirty bugger.

Harry   Don't worry. It all goes down.

Morley   Goes down?

They laugh.

Goes down where, then, lad?

Patsy   He's reporting it back, tha knows, to Moscow.

Morley   Moscow? Moscow?

Harry   Somebody does, don't you bloody worry. Everything they hear.

Fielding   Nay, Harry, lad. Thy should have warned us. (*Puts his arm round* **Harry***'s shoulder.*)

Harry   Don't worry. You carry on. (*Breaks away from* **Fielding***'s embrace.*) You'll be laughing t'other side of your bloody face. (*Exits.*)

Fielding   (*holding jersey up*)   Given me number four, an' all. I'll be all right jumping up and down i' middle o' yon bloody backs.

Kendal   By God. (*Rubbing his hands at the fire.*) I wouldn't mind being on the bloody bench today.

Pause. **Luke** *comes in, wearing a track-suit and baseball shoes and carrying a large hold-all, plus a large tin of Vaseline; sets them down by the massage table. A small, middle-aged man, perky, brisk, grey-haired.*

Fielding   Nah, Lukey, lad. Got a drop o' rum in theer, then, have you?

Luke   Aye. Could do with it today.

Morley   Lukey . . .

Kendal   Lukey . . .

Luke   Who's first on, then? (*Indicating the table.*) By Christ . . . (*Rubs his hands.*)

Patsy   My bloody shoulder . . .

Luke   Aye. Right, then. Let's have a look. (*Rummaging in his bag; gets out crêpe bandage.*)

Patsy *is stripped to his shirt by now; takes it off, hangs it and comes over in his vest and trousers. Sits on the edge of table for* **Luke** *to strap him up.*

Morley   Bloody ankle, Lukey . . .

Luke   Aye. All right.

Fielding (*examining* **Patsy**'s *shoulder*)   By God, there's nowt theer, lad. Which shoulder wa're it?

Morley   Sprained it.

Fielding   Sprained it.

Morley   Twisted it i' bed.

They laugh. **Patsy** *pays no attention. Holds his elbow as if one shoulder gives him great pain.*

Harry *comes back in with remaining jerseys.*

Luke   Right, then, lad. Let's have it off.

Having got out all his equipment, **Luke** *helps* **Patsy** *off with his vest.*

Kendal (*to* **Morley**)   Look at that, then, eh? (*Shows him his tool-kit.*) Sand-paper . . . polisher . . . circular saw . . .

Fielding (*stripping*)   What're you going to mek with that, then, Kenny?

Kendal   Dunno . . . shelves.

Morley   What for?

Kendal   Books.

Fielding (*laughs*)   Thy's never read a bleeding book.

Kendal   The wife reads . . . Got three or four at home.

Morley *laughs.*

Cupboards . . . Any amount o' things . . . Pantry door. Fitments . . .

Fielding   Fitments.

They laugh: look over at **Kendal**; *he re-examines the tools inside the parcel.*

Morley   T'only bloody fitment thy needs, Kenny . . . Nay, lad, they weern't find wrapped up inside that box.

They laugh; **Fielding** *sneezes.* **Kendal** *begins to pack up his parcel.* **Harry** *has gone out, having set the remaining jerseys. The door from the porch opens:* **Fenchurch, Jagger** *and* **Trevor** *come in.*

Fenchurch *is a neatly groomed man, small, almost dainty; wears a suit beneath a belted raincoat. He carries a small hold-all in which he keeps his boots: self-contained, perhaps even at times a vicious man.*

Jagger *is of medium height, but sturdy. He wears an overcoat, with an upturned collar, and carries a newspaper: perky, rather officious, cocky.*

Trevor *is a studious-looking man; wears glasses, is fairly sturdily built. Quiet, level-headed: a schoolmaster.*

Fielding   Fenny.

Morley   Fenchurch.

Fenchurch   Na, lad.

Jagger   Come up in old Fenny's bloody car . . . (*To* **Luke**.) By God: nearly needed thee there, Lukey . . . Blind as a bloody bat is yon . . . Old feller crossing the bleedin' road: tips him up the arse with his bloody bumper.

Fenchurch   He started coming backwards. In't that right, then, Trevor?

Trevor   Aye. He seemed to.

Luke   Did he get your name?

Jagger   Old Fenny gets out of the bleedin' car . . . How much did you give him?

Fenchurch   A bloody fiver.

Trevor   A ten-bob note.

Jagger   The bloody miser . . .

Trevor   Bends down, tha knows . . .

Jagger   He picks him up . . .

Trevor   Dusts down his coat . . .

Jagger   Asks him how he was . . . Is that right? That's all you gave him?

Fenchurch   Gone to his bloody head if I'd have given him any more.

They laugh.

Trevor (*instructional*)   You told him who you were, though, Fen.

Jagger   Offered him his bloody autograph.

They laugh.

Morley   I went up to Fenny's one bloody night . . . He said, 'I won't give you my address . . . just mention my name to anyone you see . . . ' Stopped a bobby at the end of his bloody road: 'Could you tell me where Gordon Fenchurch lives? Plays on the wing for the bloody City?' 'Who?' he said. '*Who?*' 'Fenchurch.' 'Fenchurch? Never heard of him.'

They laugh. **Fenchurch**, *taking no notice of this, has merely got out his boots and begun to examine them.*

Harry *has come in with boots.*

Jagger   Ay up, ay up. Ay up. He's here. Look what the bloody ragman's brought.

Walsh *comes in: a large, somewhat commanding figure. He wears a dark suit with a large carnation in the buttonhole. He enters from the offices, pausing in the door. He's smoking a cigar. His age, thirty-five to forty. Stout, fairly weatherbeaten. There are cries and mocking shouts at his appearance: 'Ay up, ay up, Walshy, then.' 'What's this?'*

Walsh   And er . . . who are all these bloody layabouts in here?

Fielding   The bloody workers, lad. Don't you worry.

Walsh   I hope the floor's been swept then, Harry . . . Keep them bloody microbes off my chair . . . (*Comes in.*) Toecaps polished with *equal* brightness, Harry . . . (*To* **Jagger**.) I hate to find one toecap brighter than the next.

Jagger   White laces.

Walsh   White laces.

Harry *has set the boots down. Goes out.*

Morley   Where you been, then, Walshy?

Walsh   Been?

Fielding   Been up in the bloody offices, have you? (*Gestures overhead.*)

Walsh   . . . Popped up. Saw the managing director. Inquired about the pitch . . . Asked him if they could *heat it up* . . . thaw out one or two little bumps I noticed. Sir Frederick's going round now with a box of matches . . . applying a drop of heat in all the appropriate places . . . Should be nice and soft by the time you run out theer.

Fielding   Thy's not coming with us, then?

Walsh   Nay, not for bloody me to tell . . .

Morley   It's up to more important folk than Walsh . . .

Walsh   Not more important . . . more influential . . . (*Watching* **Trevor**.) Saw you last week with one of your classes, Trev . . . Where wa're it, now, then. Let me think . . .

Trevor   Don't know.

Walsh   Quite close to the Municipal Park . . . (*Winks to* **Jagger**.) By God, some of the girls in that bloody school . . . how old are they, Trev?

Trevor   Fourteen.

Walsh   Fourteen. Could have fooled me, old lad. Could have bloody well fooled me entirely. Old Trevor: guides them over the road, you know . . . *by hand*.

Fenchurch   Where have you been, then, Walshy?

Walsh (*conscious of his carnation quite suddenly, then cigar*) Wedding.

Jagger A wedding.

Walsh Not mine . . . Sister-in-law's as a matter of fact.

Trevor Sister-in-law?

Walsh Married to me brother. Just got married a second time. Poor lass . . . Had to come away. Just got going . . . T'other bloody team's arrived . . .

Jagger Seen the bus? (*Gestures size, etc.*)

Walsh Ran over me bloody foot as near as not . . . 'Be thy bloody head next, Walsh' . . . Said it from the bloody window! . . . Said, 'Bloody well get out theer and tell me then' . . . gesturing at the field behind.

They laugh.

Load o' bloody pansies. Tell it at a glance . . . Off back theer, as a matter of fact. Going to give a dance . . . Thy's invited, Jagger, lad. Kitted out . . . Anybody else fancy a dance tonight? Champagne . . . (*Belches: holds stomach.*) I'll be bloody ill if I drink owt else . . .

Luke Thy doesn't want to let old Sandford hear you.

Walsh Sandford. Sandford . . . Drop me from this team, old lad . . . I'd gi'e him half o' what I earned.

Luke One week's dropped wages and he's round here in a bloody flash.

Walsh There was some skirt at the bloody wedding, Jagger . . . (*To* **Trevor**.) Steam thy bloody glasses up, old lad.

Jagger You're forgetting now . . . Trevor here's already married.

Walsh She coming to watch, then, Trev, old lad?

Trevor Don't think so. No.

Walsh   Never comes to watch. His wife . . . A university degree . . . what wa're it in?

Trevor   Economics.

Walsh   Economics . . . (*To* **Fenchurch**.) How do you fancy being wed to that?

Fenchurch *goes off through bath entrance.*

Jagger   Wouldn't mind being married to bloody ought, wouldn't Fenny.

Fielding   Tarts: should see the bloody ones he has.

Walsh *has warmed his hands, rubbing.*

Walsh   Kenny: how's thy wife keeping, then, old lad?

Kendal   All right.

Walsh (*looking in the parcel*)   Bought her a do-it-yourself kit, have you?

Kendal   Bought it for meself.

Morley   Going to put up one or two shelves and cupboards . . . and what was that, now?

Fielding   Fitments.

Morley   Fitments.

Walsh   By Christ, you want to be careful theer, old lad . . . Ask old Jaggers. He's very keen on fitments.

Luke   Come on, Walsh. You'll be bloody well still talking theer when it's time to be going out . . . Morley: let's have a bloody look, old lad.

Harry *has come in with last boots.*

Luke *has strapped up* **Patsy**'s *shoulder.* **Patsy** *goes back to finish changing, easing his shoulder.*

Morley *comes over to the bench: sits down on it, half-lying, his legs stretched out.* **Luke** *examines his ankle: massages with oil; starts to strap it.*

Walsh *boxes with* **Jagger**, *then goes over to his peg.*

Walsh   Sithee, Harry: I hope thy's warmed up Patsy's jersey.

Morley   Don't want him catching any colds outside . . .

They laugh. **Patsy** *has taken his jersey over to the fire to warm, holding it in front of him.*

Fenchurch (*returning*)   Seen that bloody bog?

Jagger   Won't catch Sir Frederick, now, in theer.

Fenchurch   Thy wants to get it seen to, Harry.

Harry   Has been seen to . . .

Walsh   Alus go afore I come. Drop off at the bloody peek-a-boo . . . now what's it called?

Jagger   Nude-arama.

Walsh   Best pair o' bogs this side o' town . . . Lukey, gi'e us a rub, will you, when I'm ready?

Slaps **Luke**'s *shoulder then backs up to the fire, elbowing* **Patsy** *aside.*

Luke *is strapping* **Morley**'s *ankle.*

Morley   God Christ . . . go bloody steady. (*Winces.*)

Luke   Does it hurt?

Morley   Too tight.

Trevor (*watching*)   Don't worry. It'll slacken off.

Harry *goes off.*

Fielding (*calling*)   What've you got on this afternoon, then, Jagger?

Jagger (*looking at his paper*)   A fiver.

Fielding   What's that, then?

Jagger   Two-thirty.

Walsh   Bloody Albatross.

Jagger   You what?

Walsh   Seven to one.

Jagger   You've never.

Walsh   What you got, then?

Jagger   Little Nell.

Harry *has come in with shoulder-pads and tie-ups.*

Walsh   Little Nell. Tripped over its bloody nose-bag . . . now, when wa're it . . .

Jagger   See thy hosses home, old lad.

Walsh   About ten hours after the bloody start.

They laugh.

Harry *is taking shoulder-pads to* **Jagger, Patsy, Fenchurch**, *dropping the tie-ups for the stockings on the floor, then taking the last of the shoulder-pads to Stringer's peg.* **Sandford** *has come in through the office door. He's a man of about forty, medium build; he wears an overcoat, which is now open, and carries a programme with one or two papers clipped to a pen. Stands for a moment in the door, sniffing. The others notice him but make no comment, almost as if he wasn't there.*

Sandford   I can smell cigar smoke . . . (*Looks round.*) Has somebody been smoking bloody cigars?

Walsh, *back to the fire, is holding his behind him.*

Jagger   It's Harry, Mr Sandford. He's got one here.

Walsh   That's not a bloody cigar he's got, old lad.

Harry   I don't smoke. It's not me. Don't worry.

They laugh.

Morley Come on, now, Harry. What's thy bloody got?

Harry *avoids them as* **Jagger** *sets at him. Goes.*

Sandford (*to* **Walsh**) Is it you, Ken?

Walsh Me?

Fielding Come on, now, bloody Walsh. Own up.

Walsh Wheer would I get a bloody cigar? (*Puts the cigar in his mouth; approaches* **Sandford**.) I was bloody well stopped five quid this week. Thy never told me . . . What's it for, then, Sandy?

Sandford Bloody language.

Walsh Language?

Sandford Referee's report . . . Thy wants to take that out.

Walsh Out? (*Puffs.*)

Sandford *removes it; carefully stubs it out.*

Standford You can have it back when you're bloody well dressed and ready to go home . . . If you want the report you can read it in the office.

Walsh Trevor: exert thy bloody authority, lad. Players' representative. Get up in that office . . . (*To* **Sandford**.) If there's any been bloody well smoked I shall bloody well charge thee: don't thee bloody worry . . . Here, now: let's have it bloody back.

Takes it out of **Sandford**'s *pocket, takes* **Sandford**'s *pencil, marks the cigar.*

They laugh.

Warned you. Comes bloody expensive, lad, does that.

Puts cigar back. Goes over to bench to change.

Sandford (*to* **Morley**) How's thy ankle?

Morley All right. Bit stiff.

Luke (*to* **Sandford**) It'll ease up. Don't worry.

Sandford Patsy: how's thy shoulder?

Patsy All right. (*Eases it, winces.*) Strapped it up. (*He's now put on a pair of shoulder-pads and is getting ready to pull on his jersey.*)

The others are now in the early stages of getting changed, though **Walsh** *has made no progress and doesn't intend to, and* **Fenchurch** *and* **Jagger** *are reading the racing page of the paper, still dressed.*

Harry *has come in. Puts down more tie-ups; wanders round picking up pieces from the floor, trying to keep the room tidy. The door from the porch opens and* **Copley** *comes in, limping, barging against the door. He's followed in by* **Stringer**. **Copley** *is a stocky, muscular man; simple, good-humoured, straightforward.* **Stringer** *is tall and slim; aloof, with little interest in any of the others. He goes straight to his peg and checks his kit; nods briefly to the others as he crosses.* **Copley** *staggers to the fire.*

Copley God . . . It's like a bloody ice-rink out theer . . . Christ . . . (*Pulls up his trouser-leg.*)

Sandford Are you all right . . .

Copley Just look at that.

Walsh Blood. Mr Sandford . . . Mr Sandford. Blood.

Copley You want to get some salt down, Harry . . . (*To* **Sandford**.) Thy'll have a bloody accident out theer afore tonight.

Luke *crosses over to have a look as well. He and* **Sandford** *gaze down at* **Copley**'*s knee.*

Jagger You all right, then, Stringer?

Stringer Aye.

Jagger No cuts and bruises.

Stringer No.

Morley Get nowt out of Stringer. In't that right, then, Jack?

Stringer *doesn't answer.*

Luke Well, I can't see a mark.

Copley Could'a sworn it wa' bloody cut.

Walsh   Wants to cry off there, Mr Sandford. (*To* **Copley**.) Seen the bloody pitch thy has.

Copley   Piss off.

They laugh.

Sandford (*to* **Stringer**)   Jack, then. You all right?

Stringer   Aye.

Sandford   Who else is there?

Jagger   There's bloody Owens: saw him walking up.

Fenchurch   Stopped to give him a bloody lift.

Jagger   Said he was warming up.

Walsh   Warming up!

Blows raspberry. They laugh.

Jagger   Silly prick.

Sandford (*to* **Trevor**)   You all right?

Trevor   Thanks.

Sandford   Saw your wife the other night.

Trevor   So she said.

Walsh   Ay, ay. Ay, ay . . .

Fenchurch   Heard that.

Walsh   Bloody Sandford . . .

Jagger   Coach old Trevor, Sandy, not his wife.

Sandford   It was a meeting in the Town Hall, as a matter of fact.

Walsh   Sithee – Harry: pricked up his bloody ears at that.

Fielding   What was the meeting about, then, Mr Sandford?

Sandford   Just a meeting.

Fenchurch   Town Hall, now: that's a draughty bloody place, is that.

They laugh.

Harry *goes out.*

Walsh   Come on, now, Trevor. What's it all about?

Trevor   Better ask Mr Sandford.

Walsh   He'll have no idea. Can't spell his name for a bloody start.

They laugh.

The door opens: **Atkinson** *comes in, followed by* **Spencer, Clegg** *and* **Moore.**

Atkinson   Jesus! Jesus! Lads! Look out! (*Crosses, rubbing hands, to fire.*)

Clegg   How do. How do. (*Follows him over to the fire, rubbing hands.*) By God, but it's bloody freezing.

Atkinson *is a tall, big-boned man, erect, easy-going. He wears a threequarter-length jacket and flat cap.*

Clegg *is a square, stocky, fairly small man, bare-headed, in an overcoat and scarf.*

Morley   Here you are, then, Cleggy. I've gotten the spot just here, if you want to warm your hands.

They laugh.

Spencer *and* **Moore** *are much younger men. They come in, nervous, hands in pockets.*

How's young Billy keeping, then?

Spencer   All right.

Walsh   Been looking after him, have you, Frank?

Moore   Be keeping a bloody eye on thee, then, Walsh.

Fielding   Babes in the bloody wood, are yon.

Atkinson   Here, then. I hear that the bloody game's been cancelled.

Fenchurch   Cancelled?

Copley   Cancelled?

Fenchurch   Cancelled?

Morley   Here, then, Bryan: who told you that?

Atkinson   A little bird . . .

Clegg   We were coming up . . .

Atkinson   Came over . . .

Clegg   Whispered in his ear . . .

Jagger   Give over . . .

Fenchurch   Piss off.

Copley   Rotten bloody luck.

Atkinson *and* **Spencer** *laugh.*

Sit on their bloody backsides up yonder.

Morley   Give ought, now, to have me hands in Sir Frederick's bloody pockets . . .

Walsh   Dirty bloody sod . . .

Morley   Warming. Warming . . .

Walsh   Come on, now, Sandy. Let it out. (*To* **Atkinson** *and* **Clegg**.) He's been having it off here, now, with Trevor's wife.

Trevor   All right, Walsh.

Luke   We've had enough of that.

Sandford   The meeting . . . was about . . . a municipal centre.

Jagger   A municipal what?

Fenchurch   Centre.

Clegg   Centre.

Sandford   There you are. I could have telled you.

Walsh   Sir Frederick bloody Thornton.

Jagger   What?

Walsh   Going to build it . . .

Sandford   That's right.

Walsh   Votes for it on the bloody council . . .

Jagger   Puts in his tender . . .

Sandford   He's not even on the council.

Clegg   All his bloody mates are, though.

Sandford   He asked me to attend, as a matter of fact.
There are more important things in life than bloody football.

Clegg   Not today there isn't.

Sandford   Not today there, John, you're right . . . Now,
then, Frank: are you all right?

Moore   Aye.

Sandford   Billy?

Spencer   Aye. I'm fine.

Sandford   Right. Let's have you bloody well stripped off
. . . None of you seen Clifford Owens, have you?

Moore   No.

Spencer   No . . .

Sandford (*looking at watch*)   By God: he's cutting it bloody
fine.

With varying speeds, they've all started stripping off. **Harry** *has
distributed all the kit and checked it.* **Luke**, *after strapping*
Morley*'s ankle, has started strapping* **Stringer***'s body, wrapping it
round and round with tape,* **Stringer** *standing by the table, arms held
out.*

Walsh (*to* **Sandford**)   Here, then . . . Get a bit of stuff on
. . . Let's see you do some bloody work.

Walsh *lies down on the table.*

Luke *has put his various medicine bottles from his bag by the table.*
Sandford *opens one, pours oil onto the palm of his hand and starts to
rub* **Walsh** *down.*

Kendal   Is there anywhere I can keep this, Lukey?

Copley   What you got in there, Kenny?

Morley   He's bought an electric tool-kit, Luke.

Kendal   Aye.

Fielding   Show him it, Kenny. Let him have a look.

Kendal   Drill . . . electric polisher . . . sandpaper . . .
electric saw . . . Do owt with that.

Shows it to **Copley**. **Fenchurch** *and* **Jagger** *look at it as well.*

Copley   We better tek it with us yonder, Kenny. Bloody
well mek use o' that today.

They laugh.

Stringer   I've got one of those at home.

Kendal   Oh?

Stringer   Aye.

Jagger (*winking at the others*)   Is that right, then, Jack?

Stringer   Get through a lot o' work wi' that.

Jagger   Such as?

Kendal   Bookcases.

Jagger   Bookcases?

Stringer   I've made one or two toys, an' all.

Kendal   Any amount of things.

Stringer   That's right.

Fenchurch   Who did you give the toys to, Jack?

Stringer   What?

Jagger   Toys.

Stringer   Neighbour's lad . . .

Fenchurch   Your mother fancies you, then, with one of those?

Stringer   She doesn't mind.

Copley   You ought to get together here with Ken.

Atkinson   Bloody main stand could do with a few repairs.

They laugh.

Walsh   Take no bloody notice, Jack . . . If thy's got an electric tool-kit, keep it to thysen . . . Here, then, Sandy . . . lower . . . lower!

They laugh.

By God, I could do that better, I think, mesen.

Luke   Kenny: leave it with me, old lad. I'll keep an eye on it . . . Anybody else now? Fieldy: how's thy eye?

Fielding   Be all right. A spot of bloody grease.

Luke (*to* **Copley**)   Barry. Let's have your bloody back, old lad. (*Gets out more bandage.*)

Stringer *and* **Fenchurch** *have put on shoulder-pads.* **Patsy,** *changed and ready, crosses to the mirror to comb his hair and examine himself; gets out piece of gum, adjusts socks, etc.*

The tin of grease stands on the second table by the wall. After the players have stripped, got on their shorts, they dip in the tin and grease up: legs, arms, shoulders, neck, ears. The stockings they fasten with the tie-ups **Harry** *has dropped on the floor. A slight air of expectation has begun to filter through the room: players rubbing limbs, rubbing hands together, shaking fingers, flexing; tense.*

At this point **Crosby** *comes in. He's dressed in a track-suit and enters from the office. A stocky, gnarled figure, late forties or fifties.*

Crosby   Come on . . . come on . . . half ready . . . The other team are changed already . . .

Calls of 'Ah, give over', 'Get lost', 'Silly sods', etc.

Sandford   Clifford hasn't come yet, Danny.

Crosby   He's upstairs.

Walsh   Upstairs?

Crosby (*looking round at the others, on tip-toe, checking those present*)   Bill? Billy?

Spencer (*coming out*)   Aye . . . I'm here.

Crosby   Frank?

Moore   Aye . . . I'm here.

Crosby   On the bench today, then, lads.

Sandford *slaps* **Walsh** *who gets up to finish changing.* **Clegg** *lies down to be massaged.* **Luke** *is strapping* **Copley**'s *body with crêpe bandage and strips of plaster.*

Walsh   What's old Owens doing upstairs?

Crosby   Minding his own bloody business, lad.

Clegg   Having a word with His Highness, is he?

Crosby   Patsy. How's your shoulder, lad?

Patsy   All right . . . stiff . . . (*Eases it up and down in illustration.*)

Crosby   Fieldy. How's thy eye?

Fielding   All right.

Crosby (*suddenly sniffing*)   Bloody cigars. Who the hell's been smoking?

Luke   What?

Crosby   Not ten minutes afore a bloody match. Come on.

Sandford   Oh . . . aye . . . here . . .

Crosby   You know the bloody rule in here, then, Sandy?

Sandford   Yes. Aye. Sorry. Put it out.

Luke   Is Clifford changed, then, Danny?

Crosby (*distracted*)   What?

Luke   Need a rub, or strapping up, or ought?

Crosby   Changed . . . He's gotten changed already.

Walsh   Bloody well up theer? By God, then. Bridal bloody suite is that.

Crosby   Jack? All right, then, are you?

Stringer   Fine. Aye . . . Fine. All right.

Crosby   Trevor?

Trevor   All right.

Crosby   Bloody well hard out theer. When you put 'em down . . . knock 'em bleeding hard.

Walsh   And what's Owens bloody well been up to? Arranging a bloody transfer, is he? Or asking for a rise?

They laugh.

Crosby (*reading from a list*)   Harrison's on the wing this afternoon, Patsy. Alus goes off his left foot, lad.

Patsy   Aye. Right. (*Rubs arms, legs, etc.*)

He and **Clegg** *laugh.*

Crosby   Scrum-half: new. Barry: when you catch him knock him bloody hard . . . Morley?

Morley   Aye.

Crosby   Same with you. Get round. Let him know you're theer . . . Same goes for you, Bryan.

Atkinson   Aye.

Crosby   Kenny . . . Let's see you bloody well go right across.

Morley   He's brought something to show you here, Mr Crosby.

Crosby   What?

Morley   Kenny . . . Show him your bloody outfit, Ken.

Kendal (*after a certain hesitation*)   Piss off!

They laugh.

Walsh   You tell him, Kenny, lad. That's right.

Jagger (*to* **Kendal**)   Anybody gets in thy road . . . (*Smacks his fist against his hand.*)

Clegg   Ne'er know which is bloody harder. Ground out yon or Kenny's loaf.

They laugh.

Crosby   Jack . . . Jagger . . .

Stringer   Aye.

Jagger   Aye . . .

Crosby   Remember what we said. Keep together . . . don't be waiting theer for Trev . . . If Jack goes right, then you go with him . . . Trevor: have you heard that, lad?

Trevor   Aye.

Crosby   Use your bloody eyes . . . John?

Clegg   Aye?

Crosby   Let's have a bit of bloody service, lad.

Clegg   Cliff been complaining, has he?

Crosby   Complained about bloody nowt. It's me who's been complaining . . . Michaelmas bloody Morley . . . when you get that bloody ball . . . remember . . . don't toss it o'er your bloody head.

Walsh   Who's refereeing then, old lad?

Crosby   Tallon.

Groans and cries.

Jagger   Brought his bloody white stick, then, has he?

Fenchurch   Got his bloody guide-dog, then?

Crosby (*undisturbed; to* **Copley**)   Watch your putting in near your own line, Barry . . . No fists. No bloody feet. Remember

. . . But when you hit them. Hit them bleeding hard. (*Looks at his watch.*) There's some gum. Walshy: how's thy back?

Walsh She told me, Danny, she'd never seen ought like it.

They laugh.

Crosby *drops the packets of chewing-gum on the table. Goes over to talk to the players separately, helping them with jerseys, boots, etc.*

Clegg *gets up from the table.* **Jagger** *comes to have his leg massaged by* **Sandford.**

Faint military music can be heard from outside, and the low murmur of a crowd.

Fielding *comes over to have his eye examined by* **Luke**: *he greases it over.* **Fielding** *goes back.*

Crosby Any valuables: let me have 'em . . . Any watches, ear-rings, anklets, cigarettes . . .

All Give over. Not bloody likely. Safer to chuck 'em out o' bloody winder . . .

Laughter. **Crosby, Luke** *and* **Sandford** *take valuables and put them in their pockets.*

Owens *comes in through the office door, dressed in a track-suit: bright red with 'CITY' on the back; underneath he's already changed. Medium build, unassuming, bright, about thirty to thirty-two years old, he's rubbing his hands together, cheerful. A shy man, perhaps, but now a little perky.*

Owens All right, then. Are we ready?

Jagger Sod off.

Fenchurch Give over.

Fielding Where you been?

Cries and shouts.

Harry *has come in with track-suits; gives them to* **Moore** *to give out. Goes out.*

Owens   Told me upstairs you were fit and ready. 'Just need you, Cliff,' they said, 'to lead them out.'

Walsh   And how's Sir Frederick keeping, then?

Owens   Asked me to come up a little early.

All   Ay, ay. Ay, ay. What's that? Give over.

Owens   Fill him in on the tactics we intend to use today.

Sandford   That's right.

Jagger   What tactics are those, then, Clifford?

Owens   Told him one or two hand signals he might look out for, Jag.

They laugh.

The players are picking up gum, tense, flexing. Occasionally one or other goes out through the bath entrance, returning a few moments later.

Harry *has come in with buckets and bottles of water.*

Freeze the eyeballs off a copper monkey, boy, today. By God . . . (*Goes over to the fire.*) Could do with a bit more coal on, Harry.

Sandford   You want to keep away from that bloody fire . . .

Luke   Get cramp if you stand in front of that.

Walsh   Got cramp in one place, Luke, already.

They laugh.

Owens   Just watch the ball today, boy. Come floating over like a bloody bird.

Walsh   If you listened to half he said afore a bloody match you'd never get out on that bloody field . . . Does it all, you

know, inside his bloody head . . . How many points do you
give us, then, today?

Owens   Sod all. You'll have to bloody earn 'em, lad.

Sandford   That's the bloody way to talk.

Crosby   Harry . . . where's the bloody resin board, old lad?

Jagger   Let's have a bloody ball, an' all.

Roar off of the crowd.

Harry *goes off through bath entrance.*

Morley   What bonus are we on today, then, Danny?

Crosby   All 'bonus thy'll get, lad, you'll find on t'end o' my
bloody boot . . . Now come on, come on, then, lads. Get
busy . . .

Crosby *is moving amongst the players; now all of them are almost
ready: moving over to the mirror, combing hair, straightening collars,
tightening boots, chewing, greasing ears, emptying coat pockets of
wallets, etc., and handing them to* **Crosby, Sandford** *or* **Luke.**

Tallon *comes in: a soldierly man of about forty, dressed in black
referee's shorts and shirt.*

Tallon   You all ready, then, in here?

Sandford   Aye. Come in, Mr Tallon. We're all ready, then.
All set.

Tallon   Good day for it.

Crosby   Aye. Take away a bit o' frost.

Tallon   Right. I'll have a look. Make sure that nobody's
harbouring any weapons.

A couple of players laugh.

Tallon *goes round to each player, examines his hands for rings, his
boots for protruding studs; feels their bodies for any belts, buckles or
protruding pads. He does it quickly; each player nods in greeting; one
or two remain aloof.*

As **Tallon** *goes round,* **Harry** *comes back with the resin board and two rugby balls; sets the board on the table against the wall. The players take the balls, feel them, pass them round, lightly, casual.*

Harry *moves off, to the bath entrance. He takes the coal-bucket with him.*

Owens *takes off his track-suit to several whistles; exchanges greetings, formally, with* **Tallon**.

After each player's been examined he goes over to the resin board, rubs his hands in the resin, tries the ball.

Spencer *and* **Moore** *have pulled on red track-suits over their playing-gear.*

Walsh   By God, I could do with wekening up . . . Lukey: where's thy bloody phials?

Owens   Off out tonight, then, Walshy, lad?

Walsh   I am. Two arms, two legs, one head. If you pass the bloody ball mek sure I'm bloody looking.

They laugh.

Owens   Ton o' rock there, Walshy, lad.

Walsh   Second bloody half . . . where wa're it? . . . 'Walshy! Walshy! Walshy!' . . . Passes . . . Fastening me bloody boot, what else.

Jagger   Never looks.

Walsh   Came down like a ton o' bloody lead.

They laugh.

Luke *has got out a tin of ammonia phials. The players take them, sniff, coughing, flinging back their heads; pass them on to the others. Several of the backs don't bother.* **Walsh** *takes his, breathes deeply up either nostril: no effect.*

Jagger   Shove a can o' coal-gas up theer: wouldn't make much bloody difference.

Walsh   Mr Tallon! Mr Tallon! You haven't inspected me, Mr Tallon!

They laugh. **Tallon** *comes over, finishing off.*

Tallon   All right, then, Walshy. Let's have a look.

Walsh, *arms raised, submits ponderously to* **Tallon***'s inspection.*

Walsh   Count 'em! Count 'em! Don't just bloody look.

The players laugh.

Tallon *finishes, goes over to the door.*

Tallon (*to the room*)   Remember . . . keep it clean . . . play fair. Have a good game, lads. Play to the whistle.

All   Aye. All right.

Tallon   All right, then, lads. I'll see you. May the best team win. Good luck.

An electric bell rings as **Tallon** *goes out.*

Crosby   Okay. Five minutes . . . Forr'ads. Let's have you . . . Billy? Frank? You ready?

Moore   Aye.

Spencer   Aye . . .

Crosby   Over here, then. O'd these up.

Clegg *raises his arms;* **Walsh** *and* **Fielding** *lock in on either side, casual, not much effort.*

Atkinson *and* **Kendal** *bind together and put their heads in-between the three in front.*

Fielding   Ger off. Ger off!

Walsh   A bit lower there, then, Kenny . . . Lovely. Beautiful.

Clegg   Just right.

They laugh.

Crosby (*holding the forwards with* **Spencer** *and* **Moore**)   All right. All right.

Morley *leans on* **Atkinson** *and* **Kendal**, *then, at* **Crosby**'s *signal, puts his head between them as they scrum down.*

Spencer, Moore *and* **Crosby** *are linked together.*

Let's have a ball . . . Cliff . . . Barry . . . Number four: first clear scrum we get: either side . . . (*Takes the ball* **Sandford**'s *brought him.*) Our possession, theirs . . . Clifford . . . Jagger . . . Jack . . . that's right.

The rest of the players take up positions behind: **Copley** *immediately behind, then* **Owens**, *then* **Stringer, Jagger** *and* **Patsy** *on one side,* **Fenchurch** *on the other.* **Trevor** *stands at the back.*

Right, then? Our ball, then . . .

Crosby *puts the ball in at* **Clegg**'s *feet. It's knocked back through the scrum to* **Copley**; *then it's passed, hand to hand, slowly, almost formally, out to* **Patsy**. *As each player passes it, he falls back; the scrum breaks up, falls back to make a line going back diagonally and ending with* **Fenchurch**.

Walsh   From me. To you . . .

Laughter.

Crosby   All right. All right.

When the ball reaches **Patsy** *he passes it back: to* **Jagger**, *to* **Stringer**, *to* **Owens**, *to* **Copley**, *each calling the Christian name of the one who hands it on, until it reaches* **Fenchurch**.

Walsh   Run, Fenny! Run!

Jagger   Go on. Go on! It'll be t'on'y bloody chance thy has.

They laugh.

Walsh   I never know whether it's bloody speed or fear with Fenny . . . The sound of a pair of bloody feet behind.

Walsh *catches his backside. They laugh.*

Crosby   All right. All right . . . Trev: number six.

Sandford   Come up on your positions, lads: remember that.

They get down as before, though this time **Morley** *stands out and takes* **Copley**'s *place.* **Copley** *falls back;* **Owens** *falls back behind him.* **Jagger** *and* **Patsy** *stand on one side of* **Owens**, **Stringer** *and* **Fenchurch** *on the other;* **Trevor** *stands immediately behind him.*

Crosby   Remember: first time up . . . Cliff'll give his signal . . . our head; their put in . . . doesn't matter . . .

Crosby *puts the ball in the scrum as before. The forwards play it back between their feet.* **Morley** *takes it, turns, passes it back to* **Copley**; **Copley** *passes it back to* **Owens**, **Owens** *to* **Trevor**, *who runs and mimes a drop kick.*

Jagger   Pow!

Harry *has come in with coal-bucket.*

Walsh   Now thy's sure thy won't want thy glasses, Trev?

One or two laugh.

Trevor   Just about.

Walsh   If you can't see the posts just give a shout.

They laugh.

Jagger   Walshy here'll move 'em up.

Laughter.

Crosby   All right. All right. I'll say nowt else . . .

The door from the office has already opened.

Thornton *comes in: tall, dressed in a fur-collared overcoat. A well-preserved man of about fifty.*

He's accompanied by **Mackendrick**, *a flush-faced man of about sixty. He wears an overcoat, a scarf and a dark hat.*

Thornton   Hope I'm not intruding, Danny.

Crosby   No, no. Not at all.

Thornton   Thought I'd have a word.

Sandford   That's right.

Sandford *gestures at the players. They move round in a half-circle as* **Thornton** *crosses to the centre.*

Thornton Chilly in here. That fire could do with a spot of stoking . . .

Mackendrick Harry . . . spot o' coal on that.

Harry Aye . . . Right . . . (*Mends the fire.*)

Thornton Just to wish you good luck, lads.

Players Thanks . . .

Thornton Fair play, tha knows, has always had its just rewards.

Sandford Aye . . .

Thornton Go out . . . play like I know you can . . . there'll not be one man disappointed . . . Now, then. Any grunts and groans? Any complaints? No suggestions? (*Looks round.*)

Jagger No . . .

Fenchurch No, Sir Frederick . . .

Crosby No.

Sandford No, Sir Frederick . . .

Thornton Right, then . . . Mr Mackendrick here'll be in his office, afterwards . . . if there's anything you want, just let him know . . . Good luck. Play fair. May the best team win . . . Cliff. Good luck.

Owens Thanks. (*Shakes his hand.*)

Mackendrick Good luck, Cliff . . . Good luck, lads . . .

Players Aye . . . Thanks.

Thornton Danny.

Crosby Aye. Right . . . Thanks.

Thornton Good luck, lads. See you later.

Mackendrick Danny . . .

Thornton *waves, cheerily, and followed by* **Mackendrick**, *goes.*

Silence. Broken finally by **Harry**, *stoking fire.*

Crowd roars off; fanfare music; the opposing team runs on.

A bell rings in the room.

Crosby   Right, then, lads . . . Cliff? Ought you'd like to add?

Owens   No. (*Shakes his head.*) Play well, lads . . .

Players   Aye . . .

The players, tense, nervous, start to line up prior to going out.

Owens *takes the ball. He heads the column.*

Crowd roars again; loudspeaker, indecipherable, announces names.

Walsh   Harry: make sure that bloody bath is hot.

Harry *looks across. He nods his head.*

Towel out, tha knows . . . me bloody undies ready . . .

Crosby   Bloody Walsh . . . come on. Line up . . .

Groans, moans; the players line up behind **Owens (6)**.

> **Trevor (1)**
> **Patsy (2)**
> **Jagger (3)**
> **Stringer (4)**
> **Fenchurch (5)**
> **Copley (7)**
> **Walsh (8)**
> **Clegg (9)**
> **Fielding (10)**
> **Atkinson (11)**
> **Kendal (12)**
> **Morley (13)**

Spencer (15) *and* **Moore (14)**, *in red track-suits with 'CITY' on the back, are helping* **Luke** *and* **Sandford** *collect the various pieces of equipment: spare kit, track-suits, sponges, medical bag, spare ball, bucket.*

Crosby *holds the door.*

Owens   Right, then?

All   Right. Ready. Let's get off. (*Belches, groans.*)

Crosby   Good luck, Trev . . . good luck, lad . . . good luck . . . Good luck, Mic . . .

He pats each player's back as they move out. Moments after **Owens** *has gone there's a great roar outside.*

Crosby *sees the team out, then* **Spencer** *and* **Moore** *in track-suits, then* **Luke** *and* **Sandford**. *He looks round, then he goes, closing the door.*

The roar grows louder. Music.

Harry *comes in, wanders round, looks at the floor for anything that's been dropped, picks up odd tapes, phials. Goes to the fire; puts on another piece of coal, stands by it, still. The crowd roar grows louder.*

Then, slowly, lights and sound fade.

Act Two

The same. About thirty-five minutes later.

The dressing-room is empty, the light switched off. There's a faint glow from the fire.

The roar off of the crowd: rising to a crescendo, fading.

The door from the porch opens. **Thornton** *enters, rubbing his hands, followed by* **Mackendrick**.

Thornton   By God . . . (*Gasps, shudders, stumbling round.*) Where's the light switch?

Mackendrick   Here . . .

Light switched on.

Thornton   How much longer?

Mackendrick (*looks at his watch*)   Twelve . . . fifteen minutes.

Thornton   Could do with some heating in that bloody box . . . either that or we watch it from the office. (*Crosses to the fire and warms his hands.*) Anybody in here, is there?

Mackendrick (*looks into the bath entrance*)   Don't think so.

Thornton   Got your flask?

Mackendrick   Empty. (*Shows him.*)

Thornton (*rubbing his hands*)   Send up to the office.

Mackendrick (*calls through the bath entrance*)   Harry! (*Listens: no answer. Goes to office entrance.*)

Thornton   You go, Mac . . . He'll be up in the bloody canteen, that lad. (*Has settled himself in the chair in front of the fire.*)

The crowd roars off.

Mackendrick   Shan't be a second.

Thornton   Second cabinet on the right: my office.

Mackendrick   Right. (*Hesitates, goes off through office door.*)

Thornton *settles himself in front of the fire. Crowd roars off. He raises his head, listens.*

The roar dies. He leans forward, puts piece of coal on the fire.

Door bangs off; stamping of feet; coughs, growls, clearing of throat, sighs.

Harry *comes in from the bath entrance, muffled up: balaclava, scarf, cap, ex-army overcoat, gloves.*

Harry   Oh . . . Oh . . . (*On the way to the fire sees* **Thornton** *and stops, about to go back.*)

Thornton   That's all right. Come in, Harry . . . Taking a breather.

Harry   I just nipped up to the er . . .

Thornton   That's all right, lad.

Harry   Cup o' tea.

Thornton   Pull up a chair, lad. (*Moves his own over fractionally.*)

Harry *looks round. There's no other chair. He remains standing where he is.*

Nowt like a coal fire. Hardly get it anywhere now, you know . . . Synthetic bloody fuel. Like these plastic bloody chickens. Get nought that's bloody real no more.

Harry (*sways from one foot to the other*)   Aye . . .

Thornton   Water's hot, then, is it?

Harry   What?

Thornton   For the bath.

Harry   Oh. Aye . . . (*Pause.*) I've just stoked up.

Thornton   I'd have given you a hand myself if I'd have known. By God, that box . . . like ice . . . (*Takes hands out of his gloves.*) Can't feel a thing.

Harry   It comes fro' Russia.

Thornton   What?

Harry   The cold.

Thonton   Oh . . .

Harry   East wind . . . Blows from the Russian steppes.

Thornton (*looks up*)   More north-west today, I think.

Harry   Over the Baltic . . . Norway . . .

Thornton *has raised his hand. The crowd's roar rises; he listens.*
Harry *waits. The roar dies down.*

Thornton   Them, I think . . . Score today, our lads: they'll
raise the bloody roof.

Harry   I've read it in a book.

Thornton   What?

Harry   The Russians . . . when the wind blows to the west
– spray it with a special gas.

Thornton   Good God.

Harry   Without anybody knowing . . . Breathe it . . . Take
it in . . . (*Breathes in.*) Slows down your mind . . . (*Illustrates
with limp arms and hands.*) Stops everybody thinking.

Thornton   I think our lads've had a drop of that today. By
God, I've never seen so many bloody knock-ons . . . dropped
passes . . .

Harry   I've been a workman all my life.

Thornton   Oh . . . Aye.

Harry   I used to work in a brickyard afore I came up here.

Thornton   It's a pity you're not back theer, Harry lad.
Bloody bricks we get. Come to pieces in your bloody
hand . . . Had a house fall down the other day. Know what
it was . . . ? Bricks . . . crumbled up . . . Seen nothing like
it . . . Still . . .

Harry   Knew your place before. Now, there's everybody
doing summat . . . And nobody doing owt.

Thornton   Still. Go with it, Harry.

Harry   What . . .

Thornton   Can't go against your times . . . (*Twists round.*)
Sent Mac up for a bloody snifter . . . Had time to mek the
bloody stuff by now.

Crowd's roar rises; reaches crescendo; dies. Booing.

Don't know why they do that job, you know. Refereeing.
Must have a stunted mentality, in my view. To go on with a
thing like that.

Harry   Be all communist afore long.

Thornton   Aye. (*Pokes fire.*) If the Chinese don't get here
afore.

Harry   It's happening all the time. In the mind . . . Come
one day, they'll just walk in. Take over . . . There'll be
nobody strong enough to stop them. They'll have all been
brainwashed . . . You can see it happening . . .

Thornton (*calls*)   *Mac!* Takes that man a fortnight to brew a
cup of tea. Accountant . . . He'll be up there now, counting
the bloody gate receipts. I don't think he's at all interested in
bloody football . . . He's never slow, you know, to tell us
when we've made a bloody loss.

Banging outside. **Mackendrick** *comes in with the bottle.*

Thought you'd been swigging the bloody bottle.

Mackendrick   It wasn't in the cabinet . . . I had to get it
from the bar . . . Got to sign about four receipts . . .
Anybody gets a drink in this place they bloody well deserve
it, lad.

Thornton   No glasses?

Mackendrick   Here. (*Takes two from his pocket.*)

Thornton   Was that a score?

Mackendrick   Penalty. Missed.

Thornton   Them? Or us.

Mackendrick   Seven, two. Them. It'll take some pulling back . . . Harry. (*Nods.*)

Harry   Mr Mackendrick.

Mackendrick   Wrapped up for the weather, Harry.

Harry   Aye.

Thornton   Been telling me: comes from Russia.

Mackendrick   Russia.

Thornton   Weather.

Mackendrick   Weather!

Thornton   Might have bloody guessed . . . (*To* **Harry**.) Got a cup, then, have you? Try a drop o' this.

Harry   Don't drink. Thanks all the same, Sir Frederick.

Thornton   Nay, no bloody titles here, old lad. Freddy six days o' the week. (*To* **Mackendrick**.) Sir Frederick to the wife on Sundays.

Thornton *and* **Mackendrick** *laugh.*

Thornton *drinks.*

By God. Brings back a drop of life, does that.

Mackendrick   (*drinks, gasps*)   Grand . . . Lovely.

Roar of the crowd, huge, prolonged. They listen.

Thornton   Have a look. Go on. Quick. You've missed it . . .

Mackendrick *goes to the porch; disappears outside.*

How do you think they compare to the old days, Harry?

Harry   Players? . . . Couldn't hold a bloody candle . . . In them days they'd do a sixteen-hour shift, *then* come up and lake . . . Nowadays: it's all machines . . . and they're *still* bloody puffed when they come up o' Sat'days. Run round yon field a couple of times: finished. I've seen 'em laking afore with broken arms, legs broke . . . shoulders . . . Get a scratch today and they're in here, flat on their bloody backs: iodine, liniment, injections . . . If they ever played a real team today they wouldn't last fifteen bloody seconds. That's my view. That's what I think of them today. Everywheer. There's not one of them could hold a candle to the past.

Roar and cheering from the crowd. **Thornton** *twists round and listens.*

They'll wek up one morning and find it's all too late . . .

Mackendrick *comes back in.*

Mackendrick Scored.

Thornton (*pleased*) Try?

Mackendrick Converted.

Thornton Who wa're it?

Mackendrick Morley.

Thornton By God. Bloody genius that lad.

Mackendrick *pours a drink.*

Mackendrick Harry . . . ?

Harry No thanks, Mr Mackendrick.

Thornton Harry here's been enlightening me about the past . . . Nothing like the old days, Mac.

Harry Aye!

Mackendrick Bloody bunkum.

Thornton What's that? (*Laughs: pleased.*)

Mackendrick God Christ . . . If this place was like it was twenty years ago – and that's not *too* far back – you wouldn't find me here for a bloody start . . . As for fifty years ago. Primeval . . . Surprised at thee, then, Harry lad.

Harry Aye . . . (*Turns away.*)

Mackendrick Have another snifter.

Thornton Thanks.

Mackendrick *pours it in.*

Mackendrick (*to* **Harry**)   I'd have thought thy'd see the difference, lad.

Harry *doesn't answer, turns away.*

Washed i' bloody buckets, then . . . et dripping instead o' bloody meat . . . urinated by an hedge . . . God Christ, bloody houses were nobbut size o' this – seven kiddies, no bloody bath: no bed . . . fa'ther out o' work as much as not.

Harry   There's many as living like that right now!

Mackendrick   Aye. And there's a damn sight more as not.

Thornton   I never knew you had strong feelings, Mac.

Mackendrick   About one or two bloody things I have.

He pours himself another drink. A faint roar from the crowd.

I suppose you're more on his side, then?

Thornton   Nay, I'm on nobody's bloody side, old lad . . . I had a dream the other night . . . I was telling Cliff afore the match . . . I came up here to watch a match . . . looked over at the tunnel . . . know what I saw run out? (*Laughs.*) Bloody robots. (*Laughs again.*) And up in the bloody box were a couple of fellers, just like Danny, flicking bloody switches . . . twisting knobs. (*Laughs.*) I laugh now. I wok up in a bloody sweat, I tell you.

Roar from the crowd, applause.

Noises off: boots, shouting.

Ay up. Ay up . . . (*Springs up.*)

Harry   You'll wake up one day . . . I've telled you . . . You'll wek up one day . . . You'll find it's bloody well too late.

Goes off through bath entrance.

Mackendrick   Aren't you staying to see them in?

Thornton   I'll pop in in a couple of jiffies, lad . . . You stay and give 'em a bloody cheer . . . (*Slaps his shoulder.*) Shan't be long . . . (*Calls through to bath entrance.*) Harry . . . I'll pursue that argument another time. (*Nods, winks at* **Mackendrick,** *then goes out smartly through the office door.*)

Mackendrick *moves the chair from in front of the fire just as the players start to come in.*

Fenchurch *comes in first, shaking his hand violently. He's followed by* **Luke** *carrying his bag.*

Fenchurch   Jesus! Jesus! Bloody hell.

Luke   Here . . . Let's have a look. Come on.

Jagger (*following him in*)   It's nothing . . . bloody nothing . . .

Fenchurch   Bloody studs, you see . . . Just look!

He holds it up, wincing, as **Luke** *takes it. He groans, cries out, as* **Luke** *examines it.*

The others are beginning to flood in: stained jerseys, gasping, bruised, exhausted.

Harry *brings in two bottles of water; the players take swigs from them and spit out into* **Luke**'s *bucket which* **Moore** *has carried in.*

Luke   Nothing broken. It'll be all right.

Sandford   Do you want me to bind it for you, then?

Fenchurch   No, no. No . . . No.

Jagger   Can't hold the ball with a bandage on.

Copley   Have you off to hospital, Fenny, lad. Match o'er: don't worry. Operation. Have it off. Not going to have you troubled, lad, by that.

Fenchurch   Sod off.

They laugh.

Walsh, *groaning, collapses on the bench.*

Walsh   I'm done. I'm finished. I shall never walk again. Sandy . . . Bring us a cup o' tea, old lad.

Sandford   You'll have a cup o' bloody nothing. Have a swab at that.

*Splashes a cold sponge in **Walsh***'s *face and round his neck.* **Walsh** *splutters, groans; finally wipes his face and neck.* **Crosby** *has come in with the remainder of the players.*

Crosby   Well done. Well done. Start putting on the pressure in the second half.

Jagger   Pressure?

Fenchurch   Pressure . . .

Jagger   That *was* the bloody pressure. Anything from now on is strictly left-overs, Danny lad . . . I'm knackered. Look at that. Use hammers on that bloody pitch out theer . . .

Mackendrick   Well done, then, lads. Well done.

Fielding   You watching in here, then, Mr Mackendrick, are you?

Mackendrick   Out there, old lad. I wouldn't miss it.

Clegg   See that last try . . . ?

Mackendrick   . . . Go down in the bloody book will that.

Sandford   Keep moving. Don't sit still.

Crosby   That's right. Keep moving . . . Walshy. Get up off your arse.

Walsh *takes no notice, drinks from bottle.*

Bryan? How's your ankle?

Atkinson   All right. I think. It'll be all right.

Fielding   Just look at that. Can't move me bloody finger.

Crosby   Keep away from that bloody fire . . . Sandy: keep 'em moving round, old lad.

Luke and **Sandford** *are examining individual players.* **Moore** *and* **Spencer** *are helping out with laces, tightening boots, handing round the bottles.*

Any new jerseys? Any new shorts?

A couple of players call: 'No . . . No thanks.'

Copley   Over here, lads . . . I'll have one . . .

Crosby   Trevor? How's your hands?

Trevor   All right. (*Holds them up, freezing.*)

Crosby   Keep moving, lad. Keep shifting.

Trevor   Be all right. (*He is quite cold: hands and arms folded, then rubbing himself, trying to get warm.*)

Crosby   Barry?

Copley   No. No. All right.

Stringer   Bloody cold out theer. I read it i' the paper. Seven degrees of frost last night.

Sandford   Bloody well move faster, lad.

Stringer   I am moving faster. It bloody catches up with you.

Kendal   Ears, look. Can't bloody feel 'em.

Jagger   Still on, then, Kenny, are they?

Kendal   Aye. Think so. Better have a look. (*Crosses to mirror.*)

They're gradually getting over their first shock of entering the warmer room: sucking sponges, rinsing their mouths from the bottle, rubbing on more grease, adjusting boot-fastenings and socks. Those on the move move quite slowly, tired, panting.

Fenchurch   What's the bloody score, then, lads?

Fielding   Never notices on the bloody wing.

Copley   Picking his bloody nose.

Fielding   Talking to the crowd.

Moore   Seven–seven, Fenny, lad.

Clegg (*to* **Moore** *and* **Spencer**)   Bloody cold, you lads, out theer.

Spencer   Freezing.

Moore   Fro'zen.

Walsh   Mr Crosby, sir.

Crosby   What's that?

Walsh   Isn't it time we had a substitute out theer. These lads are dying to get on and lake.

Crosby   They'll get on in *my* bloody time, not yours. Now get up. Come on. Get moving. I've told thee, Walsh, before.

Patsy *is sitting down, having his leg 'stretched' by* **Sandford**: **Patsy**'s *leg stretched out before him,* **Sandford** *pressing back the toe of his boot.*

(*To* **Patsy**.) You all right?

Patsy   Bloody cramp. God . . . (*Groans, winces.*)

Walsh   Another bloody fairy . . .

Clegg   Go on. Give him summat, Sandy . . .

Walsh   Here. Let's have a bloody hold.

Patsy   S'all right. S'all right. S'all right. (*Springs up, flexes leg.*)

Walsh   S'all in the bloody mind, tha knows . . . Here. Have a look at my bloody back, then, will you?

Sandford *lifts his jersey at the back.*

Sandford   Got a cut.

Walsh   How many stitches?

Sandford   Twenty or thirty. Can't be sure.

Walsh   Go on. Go on. Get shut . . .

Players laugh.

Fieldy: have a bloody look, old lad.

Fielding *lifts* **Walsh**'s *shirt and looks; slaps* **Walsh**'s *back.*

Walsh *goes over to the bucket, gets sponge, squeezes it down his back.*

Luke (*calling, with liniment, etc.*)   Any more for any more?

Jagger   Any bruises, cuts, concussions, fractures . . .

Copley   One down here you could have a look at, Lukey.

Opens shorts: players laugh.

Thornton *has come in from the porch entrance.*

Thornton   Well played, lads. Well done . . . Morley: bloody fine try was that, young man.

Morley   Thank you, sir.

Thornton (*to* **Crosby**)   Not often we see a run like that . . .

Crosby   No. That's right.

Thornton   Good kick, Clifford. Good kick was that.

Owens   Aye. (*During this period he has been out, through the bath entrance, to wash his face and hands, almost like an office worker set for home. Has come in now, drying face and hands.*)

Thornton   Trevor: dropped goal: a bloody picture.

Trevor   Thanks.

Thornton   How're your hands?

Trevor   Frozen.

Thornton   Saw you catch that ball: didn't know you'd got it. (*Laughs.*)

Trevor   Numb . . . (*Laughs: rubs his hands.*)

Thornton   Kenny.

Kendal *nods.*

Walsh   Sir Frederick: how d'you think I managed, then?

Thornton   Like a dream, Walshy. Like a dream.

Jagger   Bloody nightmare, I should think, more likely.

The players laugh.

Crosby   He could bloody well do wi' wekening up . . .
There's half on you asleep out yon . . . Fieldy . . . Bryan . . .
move across. Go with it . . . It's no good waiting till they come
. . . Bloody hell . . . Trevor theer: he's covering all that side
. . . Colin: *bloody interceptions*: it's no good going in, lad, every
time . . . they'll be bloody well waiting for it soon . . . three
times that *I* saw, Jack here had to take your man . . .

Walsh   Billy?

Spencer   Aye?

Walsh   Go eavesdrop at their door, old lad.

Spencer (*laughs*)   Aye!

Walsh   Find out all their plans.

They laugh.

Crosby   As for bloody Walsh. A boot up the backside
wouldn't go astray. I'll swear at times thy's running bloody
backwards, lad.

Walsh   I am. I bloody am . . . Too bloody cold today for
running forr'ad.

They laugh. **Walsh** *claps his cold hands either side of* **Sandford***'s
face.* **Sandford***, saying, 'Gerroff,' steps back.*

Crosby *goes into private, whispered conversation with individual
players.*

Mackendrick   How're you feeling, Trevor, lad?

Trevor   All right.

Mackendrick   Cut your ear there, lad . . . (*Examines it.*) Not
bad . . . Sandy? . . . Put a spot o' grease on that.

Sandford *comes across.* **Trevor** *winces.*

Take care of the professional men, you know. These lot –
(*Gestures round.*) bloody ten a penny.

Jeers. **Mackendrick** *takes no notice.*

Have you ever tried playing i' mittens, then?

Trevor   No.

Mackendrick   Some players do, you know. Particularly in your position . . . In the amateur game, you know . . . Still. No need to tell you that, I'm sure.

Trevor   Aye . . . I'll . . . just pop off in theer. Shan't be a minute.

Mackendrick   Aye . . . aye! (*Slaps his back.*)

Trevor *goes off through bath entrance.*

Electric bell rings.

Crosby   All right. All right. I'm saying no more. Quick score at the beginning: be all right . . . Cliff. At the fourth tackle, Cliff, try number five. (*To the rest.*) Have you got that?

Players   Aye.

Crosby   Be bloody ready . . . Patsy?

Patsy   Aye.

Crosby   Fenny?

Fenchurch   Aye. All right.

Crosby   Get *up* there! Bloody well stuck in.

Fenchurch   Aye.

Crosby   Bryan . . .

Atkinson   Aye.

Crosby   Harder. *Harder* . . . Kenny?

Kendal   Aye?

Crosby   *Bang 'em!* You're not tucking the buggers up in bed.

Kendal   Aye.

Crosby   Let's bloody well see it, then . . . I want to *hear* those sods go down . . . I want to feel that bloody stand start shaking . . . Johnny: have you got that, lad?

Clegg   Aye.

Crosby   Good possession . . . If their hooker causes any trouble let *Walshy* bang his head.

Walsh   I already have done, lad. Don't worry.

They laugh.

Crosby   Cliff? Ought you want to add?

Owens   No. No. Mark your man. Don't wait for somebody else to take him.

Roar of the crowd off.

They look to **Thornton**, *who's been going round to individual players, nodding formally, advising, giving praise.*

Trevor *comes back in.*

Thornton   Good luck, lads. Keep at it. Don't let the pressure drop. Remember: it's thy advantage second half. Away from home, for them: it always tells.

Crosby   Aye . . .

Thornton   Good luck.

Players (*uninterested*)   Aye . . . thanks . . .

Thornton   Go up and shake them lads out o' the bloody boardroom, Mac . . . They'll watch the match from up theer if they get half a chance . . .

Mackendrick   Aye . . . Good luck, lads. Don't let up.

Players   No . . . Aye . . .

Mackendrick   See you after. Keep it up. Well done . . . (*On his way out.*) Well done . . . Well done, Trev. (*Slaps* **Trevor**'*s back as he goes.*)

Thornton *smiles round, nods at* **Crosby**, *then follows* **Mackendrick** *out.*

Crosby   Watch Tallon near your line.

Players (*Moving off*)   Aye . . . aye.

Owens   All right, then, lads. We're off . . .

Crosby   Barry . . .

Copley (*on move out, hands clenched*)   Aye.

Crosby   Are you listening . . .

Copley   Aye. Aye. Don't worry.

Crosby   Right, then . . . Fieldy: how's thy eye?

Fielding   All right.

Crosby   It's bloody well opened. (*To* **Luke**.) Look.

Fielding   Aye. Aye. It'll be all right. (*Dismisses it, goes.*)

Crosby   Remember . . . Fenny . . . Patsy . . .

Players (*filing out*)   Aye . . . aye . . . All right.

They go. **Crosby** *nods to each one at the door, advising, slapping backs.*

Luke *and* **Sandford** *start collecting the kit to take out.* **Moore** *and* **Spencer** *still in their track-suits, pick up a bucket and a bag between them, waiting to follow* **Crosby** *out after the players have gone.*

Roar of the crowd off as the players go out.

Harry *has come in to collect the towels, tapes, bottles, etc., left lying around.*

Luke (*packing his bag*)   See you out theer, Danny . . .

Crosby   Right . . . Frank . . . Billy?

Spencer   Aye.

Crosby   Right . . .

They go.

Sandford, Luke *and* **Harry** *are left.*

Luke   Well, then, Harry . . . How's t'a barn?

Harry   All right.

Luke   Been warming up in here, then, have you?

Harry   I bloody haven't.

Sandford (*warming hands at fire*)   I'm not so sure I wouldn't prefer it here meself.

Crowd roars off.

Ay up. Ay up. That's it. We're off. (*He zips up his track-suit top, pulls his scarf round his neck.*)

Luke   Be with you in a sec, old lad.

Sandford   All right. (*Goes.*)

Luke *and* **Harry** *work in silence for a moment.*

Luke   Do you ever back on matches, Harry?

Harry   What?

Luke   Bookies.

Harry   I don't.

Luke   Nor 'osses?

Harry   Nowt.

Luke   What do you do in your spare time, then?

Harry   I don't have any spare time.

Luke   What do you do when you're not up here, then?

Harry   I'm alus up here.

Luke   Sleep up here, then, do you?

Roar off. **Luke** *raises head, listens: packs his bag.*

Harry   I sleep at home.

Luke   Where's home?

Harry   Home's in our house. That's where home is.

Luke   A damn good place to have it, lad.

Harry   Bloody keep it theer, an' all.

Luke   Thornton here, then, was he: first half?

Harry   Aye.

Luke   Crafty . . . He'll never put himself out, you know, unduly.

Harry   And Mackendrick.

Luke   Where one goes his shadder follows.

Harry It's his place . . . He can do what he likes . . . He can sit in here the whole afternoon if he bloody likes.

Luke I suppose he can.

Roar off.

F'un him up here, you know, one night.

Harry What's that?

Luke Sir Frederick . . . Came back one night . . . Left me tackle . . . Saw a light up in the stand . . . Saw him sitting theer. Alone. Crouched up. Like that.

Harry His stand. Can sit theer when he likes.

Luke Ten o'clock at night.

Harry Ten o'clock i' the bloody morning. Any time he likes.

Luke *fastens his bag.*

Luke Is it true, then, what they say?

Harry What's that?

Luke Thy's never watched a match.

Harry Never.

Luke Why's that?

Harry My job's in here. Thy job's out yonder.

Luke They ought to set thee on a pair o' bloody rails. (*Goes over to the door.*)

Harry Most jobs you get: they're bloody nowt . . .

Luke *pauses at the door.*

Don't know what they work for . . .

Luke What?

Harry Not any more. Not like it was . . .

Luke Well, thy works for the bloody club.

Harry I work for Sir Frederick, lad: for nob'dy else.

Luke *looks across at him.*

I mun run the bloody bath. (*He goes.*)

Luke *watches from the door, then looks round for anything he's forgotten. Comes back in, gets scissors. Sound off, from the bath entrance, of running water. He crosses to the door and goes.*

Harry *comes back a moment later. He gets towels from the basket and lays them out on the bench, by each peg. At one point there's a roar and booing from the crowd, trumpets, rattles. It dies away to a fainter moan.* **Harry** *turns on the Tannoy.*

Tannoy (*accompanied by roaring of the crowd*) ' . . . Copley . . . Clegg . . . Morley . . . Fenchurch! . . . inside . . . passes . . . Jagger . . . Stringer . . . Tackled. Fourth tackle. Scrum down. Walsh . . . Fielding . . . Walsh having words with his opposite number! Getting down. The scrum is just inside United's half . . . almost ten yards in from the opposite touch . . . put in . . . some rough play inside that scrum . . . Referee Tallon's blown up . . . free kick . . . no . . . scrum down . . . not satisfied with the tunnel . . . ball in . . . Walsh's head is up . . . (*Laughter.*) There's some rough business inside that scrum . . . my goodness! . . . Ball comes out . . . Morley . . . Copley . . . Owens . . . Owens to Trevor . . . *Trevor is going to drop a goal* . . . too late . . . He's left it far too late . . . They've tried that once before . . . Kendal . . . '

Harry *switches the Tannoy off.*

Great roar outside.

Harry *has crossed to the fire; more coal; pokes it. Goes off to the bath entrance.*

A moment later the door from the porch opens: **Sandford** *comes in.*

Sandford (*calling*) Luke? . . . Luke?

Harry (*re-emerging*) He's just gone . . .

Sandford Oh, Christ . . .

Harry Anything up?

Sandford Gone through the bloody tunnel . . . Missed him.

Roar increasing off. **Sandford** *hurries out.* **Harry** *stands in the centre of the room waiting. Baying of the crowd. A few moments later, voices off:* 'Hold the bloody door.' 'This side.' 'This side.' 'Take his shoulder.' 'I'm all right. I'm all right. Don't worry.'

The door opens: **Kendal** *comes in, supported by* **Crosby** *and* **Moore**.

Kendal   It's all right . . . It's bloody nowt . . . Where is it? Where's he put it?

Crosby   Get him down . . . no, over here. Over here. On this.

They take him to the massage table.

Kendal   Now, don't worry. Don't worry . . . Don't worry. I'll be all right . . .

Moore   S'all right, Kenny, lad. All right.

Crosby   Doesn't know where he is . . . Now, come on. Lie down, Kenny, lad. Lie down.

Kendal   S'all right. S'all right.

Crosby   Where's bloody Lukey . . . Frank: get us a bloody sponge. Harry: o'd him down.

Crosby *tries to hold* **Kendal** *down: having been laid on the table, he keeps trying to sit up.*

Harry *comes over to the table. He watches, but doesn't help.*

Harry (*to* **Moore**)   Over theer . . . that bucket.

Moore *goes off to the bath entrance.*

Crosby   Come on, Kenny. Come on . . . Lie down, lad.

Kendal   S'all right . . . S'all right . . . I'll go back on.

Crosby   You'll go nowhere, lad . . . Come on . . . Come on, then, Kenny, lad. Lie still. I want to bloody look . . . Come on . . .

The door opens: **Sandford** *comes in, followed by* **Luke** *with his bag.*

Luke How is he? . . . Don't move him . . . Let's have a look.

Crosby Where's thy been? . . . On thy bloody holidays, hast tha?

Luke Let's have a look . . . I was coming up . . .

Crosby Nose . . .

Steps back, **Sandford** *takes hold.*

Crosby *gets a towel, wipes his hands.*

Kendal Nose . . . It's me nose, Lukey . . .

Luke Lie still, lad, now. Lie still.

Kendal I can't bloody see, Lukey . . .

Luke Now just lie still . . . That's it . . . That's right . . .

Moore *has brought the sponge.*

Get some clean water, lad. That's no good . . .

Sandford Here . . . here . . . I'll get it. (*To* **Moore**.) Come round here. Get o'd o' this.

Moore *takes* **Sandford**'s *place.*

Sandford *goes off to bath entrance.*

Luke *has looked at* **Kendal**'s *wound.* **Kendal**'s *face is covered in blood.* **Luke** *sponges round his cheeks and mouth, then stoops down to his bag, gets out cotton wool.* **Kendal** *is still trying to get up.*

Moore It's all right, Kenny, lad. All right.

Kendal Can't see . . .

Luke Now just keep your eyes closed, lad . . . Harry: can you get a towel?

Moore I don't think Ken wa' even looking . . . His bloody head came down . . . bloody boot came up . . .

Harry *has passed over a towel.* **Moore** *takes it.*

Luke Shove it underneath his head . . . Kenny? Keep your head still, lad.

Sandford *has brought in a bowl of water.*

Luke *wipes away the blood with cotton wool, examines the damage.* **Sandford** *pours a drop of disinfectant from the bottle into the bowl of water.* **Luke** *dips in the cotton wool, wipes* **Kendal**'s *nose.*

Crosby, *not really interested, having wiped the blood from his hands and his track-suit, looks on impatiently over* **Luke**'s *back.*

Kendal A bit o' plaster: I'll go back on.

Luke Nay, lad. The game's over for you today.

Kendal I'll be all right . . . I'll get back on . . .

Crosby He's off, then, is he?

Luke Aye . . .

Sandford Aye . . . (*Gestures up.*) I'll take him up.

Crosby Right . . . Frank. Come on. Not have you hanging about down here.

Sandford Who you sending on?

Crosby (*looks round; to* **Frank**) Do you think you can manage, then, out theer?

Moore Aye!

Crosby Come on, then. Let's have you up.

Moore, *quickly, jubilantly, strips off his track-suit.*

Lukey . . .

Luke Aye.

Crosby   As soon as you've done. Let's have you up . . .
Kenny: do you hear that, lad?

Kendal (*half-rising*)   Aye . . .

Crosby   Well done, lad . . . Just do as Lukey says . . .

Kendal   Aye . . .

Crosby (*to* **Moore**)   Come on. Come on. Not ready yet . . .

Has gone to the door. **Moore** *scrambles out of the suit.* **Crosby** *goes.*
Moore, *flexing his legs, pulling down his jersey, etc., hesitates.*

He goes.

Luke   Theer, then, Kenny . . .

Luke *has finished washing the wound and has dressed it with a
plaster. He now helps* **Kendal** *up with* **Sandford**'s *assistance.*

If there's ought you want, just give a shout.

Kendal   There's me electric tool-kit, Luke . . .

Luke   I've got it here, old lad . . . Thy'll be all right . . .

Kendal   Fifteen quid that cost . . . just o'er . . .

Sandford   Here, then. Come on . . . Let's have you in the
bath. Come on. Come on, now . . . It wouldn't do you much
good if you dropped it in . . .

Kendal *has got up from the table.*

Sandford *helps him over to the bath entrance.*

Luke *finishes packing his bag.*

The porch door opens: **Mackendrick** *comes in.*

Mackendrick   How is he?

Luke   He'll be all right.

Mackendrick   Too bloody old, you know. If I've said it
once, I've said it . . .

Luke   Aye.

Mackendrick (*calls through*) How're you feeling, Kenny, lad.

Kendal (*off*) All right.

Mackendrick All right, Sandy?

Sandford (*off*) Aye. I'll have him in the bath.

Mackendrick Taking him up . . . ? (*Gestures up.*)

Sandford (*off*) Aye.

Mackendrick I'll see about a car.

Sandford (*off*) Shan't be long.

Mackendrick (*to* **Luke**) I'll go up to the office.

Luke Tool-kit. (*Shows him.*)

Mackendrick *looks in.*

Bloody shelves . . .

Mackendrick Poor old Kenny . . .

Luke Bloody wife.

Mackendrick Like that, then, is it?

Luke Been round half the teams i' the bloody league . . . one time or another. (*Packs his bag and goes over to the bath entrance.*) I'll get on up, then, Sandy, lad.

Sandford (*off*) Aye.

Luke Be all right, then, Kenny, lad?

Kendal (*off*) Aye . . .

Luke *collects his bag.*

Luke You'll see about a taxi, then?

Mackendrick Aye.

Roar off.

They lift their heads.

Luke Another score.

Mackendrick (*gestures at bath entrance*)   I'll get up and tell Sir Freddy, then.

Mackendrick *goes out by the office entrance,* **Luke** *by the porch.*

Harry *is left alone. He's cleared up the bits of cotton wool and lint; he collects the used towels.*

Sandford *brings in* **Kendal**'s *used kit, drops it on the floor. Gets a towel.*

Sandford   Take care of that, then, Harry . . .

Harry   Aye.

Sandford   Them his clothes?

Harry   Aye.

Sandford *gets them down. He goes to the bath entrance with the towel.*

Sandford (*off*)   Come on, then, Kenny . . . Let's have you out.

Harry *retidies the massage table, resetting the head-rest which, for* **Kendal**'s *sake, has been lowered.*

A moment later **Kendal**'s *led in with a towel round him.*

Can you see ought?

Kendal   Bloody dots . . .

Sandford   No, this way, lad, then. Over here.

Kendal   Is the game over, Sandy . . . ?

Sandford   Just about. Sit theer. I'll get you dried . . .

Kendal *sits on the bench.* **Sandford** *dries his legs and feet, then he dries his head.*

Harry *looks on.*

Pass his shirt, then, will you?

Harry *passes* **Kendal**'s *shirt and vest over.*

There's a roaring of the crowd off.

Kendal   Are we winning?

Sandford   Come on, then . . . Get your head in this.

Kendal   Can't remember . . .

Sandford *pulls his vest and shirt round his head.* **Kendal** *dazedly pushes in his arms.*

Harry   What's he done?

Sandford   Nose.

Harry   Bro'k it, has he?

Sandford   Aye.

Kendal   Remember shopping.

Sandford   We've got it here, old lad. Don't worry.

Kendal   Bloody fifteen quid . . .

Harry   F'ust one this year.

Sandford   Come on, then, lad . . . Let's have you up.

Sandford *helps* **Kendal** *to his feet.* **Harry** *watches, hands in pockets.* **Kendal** *leans on* **Sandford. Sandford** *pulls on his trousers.*

Harry   Three collar-bones we had one week . . . Two o' theirs . . . the last un ours . . . Ankle . . . Bloody thigh-bone, once . . . Red hair . . . He never played again.

Sandford (*to* **Kendal**)   Come on, come on, then, lad . . . o'd up.

Kendal   Steam-boilers, lad . . . Bang 'em in . . . Seen nothing like it. Row o' rivets . . . Christ . . . Can hardly see ought . . . Sandy?

Sandford   Here, old lad. Now just hold tight . . . Come on. Come on, now. Let's have you out of here . . . (*To* **Harry**.) Will you see if Mr Mackendrick's got that car? . . . (*As* **Harry** *goes.*) Harry: can you find me coat as well?

Harry *goes, stiffly, leaving by office entry.*

Roar off, rises to peak, applause, bugles, rattles.

Kendal *turns towards sound, as if to go.*

Nay, lad: can't go with nothing on your feet.

Sits **Kendal** *down, puts on his socks and shoes.*

Kendal (*dazed*)   Started lakin' here when I wa' fifteen, tha knows . . . Intermediates . . . Then I went out, on loan, to one of these bloody colliery teams . . . bring 'em up at the bloody weekend in bloody buckets . . . play a game o' bloody football . . . booze all Sunday . . . back down at the coalface Monday . . . Seen nothing like it. Better ring my wife.

Sandford   What?

Kendal   She won't know.

Sandford   She's not here today, then?

Kendal   No . . .

Sandford   I'll see about it, lad. Don't worry.

Kendal   If I'm bloody kept in, or ought . . .

Sandford   Aye. It'll be all right.

Kendal   The woman next door has got a phone.

Sandford   Aye. I'll see about it, lad. All right. (*Gets up.*) Let's have your coat on. Won't bother with your tie.

Kendal *stands.* **Sandford** *helps him into his raincoat.*

Kendal   I wa' going to get a new un . . . until I bought this drill . . .

Sandford   Aye! (*Laughs.*)

Kendal   Start saving up again . . .

Sandford   That's right.

Harry *comes in through the office door. He brings in* **Sandford**'s *overcoat.*

Harry   There's one outside already.

Sandford   Good.

Harry (*watches* **Sandford**'s *efforts*) Alus one or two out theer.

Sandford Yeh.

Harry Sat'days.

Sandford Could alus use Sir Frederick's, then.

Harry Aye . . .

Sandford How're you feeling, lad?

Kendal All right.

Sandford Come on, then, lad . . . Just fasten this . . .

Kendal *holds his head up so* **Sandford** *can fasten on the dressing Luke has left. It covers his nose and is fastened with plaster to his cheeks.*

Kendal Is it broke?

Sandford There's a bit of a gash, old lad.

Kendal Had it broken once before . . .

Sandford Can you manage to the car? (*Collects his coat.*)

Kendal Wheer is it, then? (*Turns either way.*)

Sandford Here it is, old lad . . . (*Hands him his parcel.*)

Kendal Have to get some glasses . . . hardly see . . .

Sandford (*to* **Harry**) Looks like bloody Genghis Khan . . . Come on, then, Kenny . . . Lean on me. (*To* **Harry**.) Still got me bloody boots on . . . I'll get them in the office . . . See you, lad.

Harry *watches them go.*

He waits. Then he picks up the used towel, takes it off to dump inside the bath entrance.

He comes back, looks round, switches on the Tannoy.

Tannoy (*crowd roar*) ' . . . to Walsh . . . reaches the twenty-five . . . goes down . . . plays back . . . (*Roar.*) . . . Comes to

Clegg to Atkinson . . . Atkinson to the substitute Moore . . .
Moore in now, crashes his way through . . . goes down . . .
Walsh comes up . . . out to Owens . . . Owens through . . .
dummies . . . beautiful move . . . to Stringer, Stringer out to
Patsy . . . Patsy out to Trevor, who's come up on the wing
. . . kicks . . . Copley . . . Fenchurch . . . Fielding . . . *Morley*
. . . (*Roar.*) Ball bounces into touch . . . scrum . . . (*Pause, dull
roar.*) Growing dark now . . . ball goes in, comes out, Tallon
blows . . . free kick . . . scrum infringement . . . one or two
tired figures there . . . can see the steam, now, rising from
the backs . . . Trevor's running up and down, blowing in his
hands . . . Kick . . . good kick . . . (*Crowd roar.*) Finds touch
beyond the twenty-five . . . (*Crowd roar.*)

Harry *sits, listening.*

Fade: sound and light.

Act Three

The same.

Noise: shouting, singing, screeching, cries off. The Tannoy is playing music.

Patsy, *a towel round his waist, is drying himself with a second towel, standing by his clothes. He does it with the same care with which he prepared himself for the match.*

Harry *is picking up the mass of discarded shorts, jerseys, jock-straps, and putting them on the basket.*

A pile of towels stands on the rubbing-down table.

Spencer *is half-dressed in trousers and shirt, combing his wet hair in the mirror.*

Crosby *is going round checking boots, putting pairs together by the massage table to be collected up.*

Crosby (*to* **Spencer**)   Up there waiting for you, is she, Billy?

Spencer   Aye. All being well. (*Combing in mirror.*) Bloody expecting me to play today, an' all.

Crosby   Ne'er mind. Next week: might be in luck.

Spencer   Bloody away next week!

Crosby   Maybe she'll have to bloody travel.

Spencer   Not the travelling kind, you know.

Crosby   Can't win 'em all, old lad. Don't worry . . . (*Calls.*) Come on. Let's have you out o' there . . . (*Switches off Tannoy, moves on. To* **Patsy**.) How're you feeling, then, old lad?

Patsy   All right. Bit stiff. (*Winces: eases arm.*)

Crosby   How's thy shoulder?

Patsy   All right.

Crosby   Bloody lovely try. Worth any amount o' bloody knocks is that.

Patsy   Aye.

Crosby   Couple more next week . . . should be all right.

Patsy   Aye. (*Doesn't respond, drying himself, turns to check his clothes.*)

Jagger *comes bursting in from the bath.*

Jagger   Dirty bugger . . . dirty sod . . . Danny: go bloody stop him. (*Snatches towel, rubs his hair vigorously.*) Walshy – pittling in the bloody bath.

Spencer (*calling through*)   Thy'll have to disinfect that bloody water . . . (*Laughing.*)

Walsh (*off*)   This *is* disinfectant, lad.

Crosby   Come on, Walshy: let's have you out . . .

Takes a towel and dries **Jagger**'s *back.*

Jagger   Dirty bugger: dirty sod!

Walsh (*off*)   Come on, Jagger. You could do with a bloody wash.

Jagger   Not in that, you dirty sod . . . Set bloody Patsy onto you, if you don't watch out.

Water comes in from the bath.

Dirty! Dirty! . . .

Dances out of the way: laughter and shouting off.

Crosby   Come on, Trevor. Teach 'em one or two manners, then . . . Bloody college-man . . . going to go away disgusted with all you bloody working lads.

Another jet of water. **Crosby** *lurches out of the way.*

Bloody well be in there if you don't watch out.

Jeers, cries.

Copley (*off*)   Too bloody old!

Clegg (*off*)   Come on, Danny. Show us what you've got.

Crosby   Get summat here that'll bloody well surprise you, lad . . .

Laughter, cries.

And you!

Laughter off.

Sithee . . . Billy. Go in and quieten 'em down.

Spencer   Nay . . . gotten out in one bloody piece. Not likely. Send Harry in. He'll shift 'em out.

Harry *looks up: they laugh. He doesn't respond.*

Singing starts off, then all join in from the bath.

Luke *comes in.*

Crosby   Got through, then, did you?

Luke   He'll be all right . . .

Jagger   Kenny?

Luke   Broken nose.

Jagger   Keeping him in, then, are they?

Luke   Aye.

Jagger   Give his missus chance to bloody roam.

Luke (*goes over to* **Patsy**)   How's it feel, old lad?

Patsy   All right. (*Eases his shoulder, stiffly.*)

Luke   Come in tomorrow: I'll give you a bloody rub.

Patsy   Right.

Luke   Need a drop of stuff on theer. (*Goes to his bag.*)

Trevor *has come in, wiping himself down with a towel.*

Trevor   Just look . . . just beginning to get up circulation . . .

Flexes his fingers.

Jagger   Circulate a bit lower down for me.

Crosby *has a towel and now dries* **Trevor**'s *back.*

Trevor Bloody shaking, still. Just look. (*Holds out his hands, trembling.*)

Crosby Don't worry. This time tomorrow . . .

Flicks towel to **Spencer**, *who finishes rubbing* **Trevor***'s back.*

Spencer What's thy teach, then, Trev?

Trevor Mathematics.

Spencer Maths . . .

Trevor One of your subjects, is it?

Spencer One . . . (*Laughs.*)

Luke T'other's bloody lasses, Trev.

Spencer Nay, I gi'e time o'er to one or two other things, an' all.

They laugh.

Jagger Here . . . Got the two-thirty, Lukey, have you?

Luke Somewheer . . . (*Tosses the paper over from his pocket.*)

Spencer (*to* **Trevor**) That kind o' mathematics, Trev.

Slaps **Trevor***'s back: finished drying.*

Trevor Shoulda known. (*Turns away to get dressed.*)

Jagger Let me see . . . (*Examines stop-press.*) One-thirty . . . (*To* **Spencer**.) Quite a bit fastened up in that . . . (*Reading.*) Two o'clock . . . Two-thirty . . . No . . .

Crosby What's that, Jagger, lad?

Jagger *tosses paper down. Goes to his clothes.*

Spencer Let's have a look.

Jagger (*to* **Luke**) Don't say a word to bloody Walsh.

Luke Shan't say a word. (*Laughs.*) Not a sausage.

Luke *has dabbed an orange-staining antiseptic on* **Patsy**'s *arm; now he crosses to* **Trevor**. *As* **Trevor** *starts to dress he moves round him, dabbing on antiseptic with cotton wool.*

Hold still. Hold still.

Clegg *comes in, drying.*

Clegg   Bit lower down there, Lukey.

Luke   Aye. (*Laughs.*)

Spencer (*reading*)   Bloody Albatross. Seven to one.

Jagger   What d'you back, Billy, lad?

Spencer   Same as you, Jag. Little Nell. (*To* **Luke**.) Tipped the bloody 'oss himself.

Jagger   Bloody Walsh . . . Never hear the end.

Clegg   What's that?

Jagger, *dry, has started to dress.* **Spencer** *has taken the towel from* **Clegg** *and is drying his back.*

Jagger   Albatross: come up . . . (*Gestures off.*)

Clegg (*to* **Spencer**)   What's that?

Spencer   I'm saying nowt.

Flicks the towel to **Clegg**, *picks up another.*

Copley *has come in, followed by* **Fenchurch**. **Spencer** *goes to dry* **Copley**'s *back,* **Crosby** *to dry* **Fenchurch**'s.

Copley   Sithee, there ought to be a special bloody bath for those dirty bloody buggers: I'm muckier now than when I bloody well went in.

Walsh (*off, siren-call*)   Barry! Barry! *We can't do without you, Barry!*

Copley (*calling*)   Sod off.

Morley (*siren, off*)   Barr . . . y!

Walsh (*siren, off*)   Barr . . . y . . .

Morley (*off*)   Barr . . . y! . . . We're *waiting*, Barry!

Copley (*calling*)   Piss off!

Crosby   Come on, Fieldy . . . Keep those ignorant sods in line.

Fielding (*off*)   I'm in the bloody shower. I'm not in with those mucky bloody sods.

Jagger   How're you feeling, Fenny, lad?

Fenchurch   All right . . . (*Indicating paper.*) Results in theer, then, are they?

Clegg (*has picked it up to read*)   Aye. (*Reads.*) 'Latest score: twelve-seven.' Patsy: they didn't get thy try . . . Sithee: pricked up his bloody ears at that.

They laugh. **Patsy**, *having turned, goes back to dressing.*

Fenchurch   Fifteen-seven . . .

Jagger   Fifteen-seven.

Fenchurch   Put a good word in with Sir Frederick, then.

Crosby   Good word about bloody what, then, lad?

Fenchurch   Me and Jagger, Danny boy . . . Made old Patsy's bloody try . . . In't that right, then, Jagger lad?

Patsy   Made me own bloody try. Ask Jack . . .

Stringer *has come in, shaking off water.* **Crosby** *goes to him with a towel: dries his back.*

Morley (*off*)   Any more for any more?

Laughter off.

Walsh (*off*)   Barry . . . y! *We're waiting, Barry!*

Fenchurch   Take no notice. Silly sod.

Stringer   Where's Cliff, then?

Jagger   Up in the directors' bath, old lad.

Stringer   Is that right, then?

Crosby   Captain's privilege, lad.

Stringer   Bloody hell . . . (*Snatches towel, goes over to the bench to dry himself.*)

Luke *is still going round, dabbing on antiseptic.*

Luke   Any cuts, bruises: ought that needs fastening up?

Jagger   I've a couple of things here that need a bit of bloody attention, Lukey . . .

Luke   What's that?

Goes over; **Jagger** *shows him.*

They all laugh.

Patsy *has crossed to the mirror to comb his hair.*

Patsy   Did you see a young woman waiting for me up there, Danny?

Groans and jeers from the players.

Clegg   How do you do it, Patsy? I can never make that out.

Fenchurch   Nay, his girl-friend's a bloody schoolmistress. Isn't that right, then, Patsy?

Patsy *doesn't answer: combs his hair, straightens his tie.*

Jagger   Schoolmistress?

Fenchurch   Teaches in Trevor's bloody school . . . Isn't that right, then, Trev?

Trevor *nods, doesn't look up: gets on with his dressing.*

Jagger   What do you talk about, then, Patsy?

They laugh. **Patsy** *is crossing to his coat. With some care he pulls it on.*

Clegg (*having gone to him*)   The moon in *June* . . . Is coming out quite *soon!*

Walsh (*off*)   Barr . . . y! *Where are you, Barr . . . y!*

Copley   Piss off, you ignorant sod.

Morley (*off*)   Barr . . . y! *We're waiting, Barr . . . y!*

Laughter off.

Luke Sithee . . . Can you sign these autograph books: there's half a dozen lads outside . . . Clean forgot. (*Takes them from his pocket, puts them on the table.*)

Jagger By God: just look at that!

Patsy *has already crossed to the table.*

Pen out in a bloody flash . . .

Patsy *takes out a pen clipped to his top pocket. Writes.* **Jagger** *stoops over his shoulder to watch.*

He can write, an' all . . . 'Patrick Walter Turner.' Beautiful. Bloody beautiful is that.

Patsy Piss off.

Jagger Here, now. Bloody language, Trev! . . . Hears that, she'll never speak again.

Fenchurch Put you down in her bloody book . . .

Jagger Black mark.

Fenchurch A thousand lines . . .

Jagger 'I must not bloody swear, you cunt.'

They laugh.

Fielding *comes in, picks up a towel.* **Spencer** *goes over to dry his back.*

Fielding They're going to be in theer a bloody fo'tnight . . . Harry – go in and pull that bloody plug.

Harry Aye. (*Doesn't look up.*)

Burst of laughter. Shouts off: 'Give over! Give over! You rotten bloody sod!'

Stringer They could do with putting in separate bloody showers in theer.

Crosby What's that, Jack?

Stringer Separate showers. It's not hygienic, getting bathed together.

Clegg It's not. He's right. That's quite correct.

Fenchurch Put a bit o' colour in your cheeks, old lad.

Stringer I've got all the colour theer I need.

Jagger Played a grand game today, though, Jack. (*Winks at the others.*)

Stringer Aye. (*Mollified.*)

Jagger Marvellous. Bloody fine example, that.

Stringer Aye. Well . . . I did my best.

Jagger Them bloody forwards: see them clear a way.

They laugh. **Stringer** *dries his hair, rubbing fiercely.*

Atkinson *comes in from the bath, limping.*

Crosby *gets a towel, dries his back.*

Luke Let's have you on here, Bryan. Let's have a look.

Luke *waits by the table while* **Atkinson** *gets dry.*

Morley (*off*) Barry! *Where are you, Barry!*

Walsh (*off*) Barry! *We're waiting, Barry . . .*

Copley *looks round: sees one of the buckets: takes it to the bath entrance: flings the cold water in.*

Cries and shouts off.

The players laugh.

Crosby Go on. Here . . . Here's a bloody 'nother.

Copley *takes it, flings the water in.*

Cries, shouts off.

The players laugh, looking over at the bath entrance.

Atkinson *is dry now and, with a towel round him, he lies down on the massage table.* **Luke** *examines his leg.*

Patsy, *having got on his coat, has returned to the mirror. Final adjustments: collar, tie, hair . . .*

Stringer *continues getting dressed.* **Trevor** *joins* **Patsy** *at the mirror.*

Fenchurch, Jagger *and* **Clegg** *are almost dressed,* **Fielding** *just beginning.*

Jagger   Go on, Barry! Ought else you've bloody got!

Copley *looks round, sees nothing.*

Crosby   Here . . . Come on . . . Turn on that bloody hose.

He picks up the end of the hose by the bath entrance, turns the tap. They spray the water into the bath entrance.

Cries and shouts from the bath.

The players call out: 'More! More! Go on! All over!'

Cries and shouts off. A moment later **Moore** *and* **Morley** *come running in, shaking off water, the players scattering.*

Moore   Give over! Give over! Ger off!

They grab towels, start rubbing down.

Walsh (*off*)   More! More! Lovely! Lovely! . . . That's it, now, lads . . . No. No. Right . . . Lovely. Lovely . . . Bit lower, Barry . . . Lovely! Grand!

The players laugh.

Crosby (*to* **Copley**)   All right . . .

Luke   That's enough . . .

Crosby   Nowt'll get through that bloody skin, I can tell you. (*Calls through.*) We're putting the lights out in ten minutes, lad . . . You can stay there all night if tha bloody wants.

Copley *turns off the tap.*

The players go back to getting dressed.

Stringer   All over me bloody clothes. Just look.

Fielding   Here . . . here, old lad. I'll mop it up . . . Grand game today, then, Jack.

Stringer   Aye . . . All right.

Crosby dries **Moore***'s back,* **Spencer** *dries* **Morley***'s.*

Crosby   What's it feel like, Frank?

Moore   Grand . . . Just got started.

Fielding   Knows how to bloody lake, does Frank . . . ten minutes . . .

Moore   Nearer thi'ty.

Fielding   Just time to get his jersey mucky . . .

Crosby   He'll bloody show you lads next week . . .

Fielding   Can't bloody wait to see, old lad.

Walsh (*off*)   Barry . . . *I'm waiting*, Barry!

The players laugh.

Copley   Well, I'm bloody well not waiting here for thee!

They laugh.

The door from the office has opened.

Thornton, *followed by* **Mackendrick**, *comes in.*

Thornton   Well done, lads . . . Bloody champion . . . well done . . . They'll not come here again in a bloody hurry . . . not feel half so bloody pleased . . . How's thy feeling, Patsy, lad?

Patsy   All right, sir.

Thornton   Lovely try . . . Bloody textbook, lad . . . Hope they got that down on bloody film . . . Frank? How's it feel, young man?

Moore   Pretty good. All right.

Crosby   Just got started . . .

Fielding   Just got into his stride, Sir Frederick.

Thornton Another ten minutes . . . he'd have had a bloody try.

They laugh.

Set 'em a bloody fine example, lad, don't worry. Well played there, lad. Well done.

Mackendrick Well done, lad.

Thornton How's your leg, then, Bryan?

Atkinson Be all right.

Atkinson *is still on the table.* **Luke** *is massaging the leg with oil.*

Thornton Nasty bloody knock was that.

Atkinson Went one way . . . Me leg went t'other.

Thornton (*to* **Trevor**) How's your hands now, then, lad?

Trevor All right. Fine, thanks. (*Has pulled on his club blazer. Looks up from dusting it down.*)

Thornton (*to* **Fielding**) I hope you're going to get your eye seen to there, old lad.

Fielding Aye.

Thornton Bad news about old Kenny.

Players Aye . . .

Walsh (*off*) Barr . . . y . . . I am *waiting*, Barry!

Thornton Who's that, then? Bloody Walsh?

Crosby Aye.

Thornton (*going to the bath entrance*) And who's thy waiting for, then, Walshy?

Pause.

Walsh (*off*) Oh, good evening, Sir Frederick . . .

Thornton I'll give you Sir bloody Frederick . . . I'll be inside that bath in a bloody minute.

Walsh (*off*) Any time, Sir Frederick, any time is good enough for me.

The players laugh.

Mackendrick *has moved off amongst the players, going first to* **Patsy**, *then to* **Trevor**, *slapping backs: 'Well done. Good match.'*

Thornton *turns back to the players.*

Thornton I think we ought to charge Walsh bloody rent: spends more time here than he does at home.

Crosby Thy had five quid off him here last week: swearing to the referee.

Mackendrick That's right. We did!

They laugh.

Thornton No luck this week, then, I fancy?

Crosby Shouldn't think so. Tallon's not above bloody answering back.

Thornton Shifty bugger is old Walshy . . . Grand try in the first half, Mic. Good game.

Morley Thanks.

Morley, *his back dried by* **Spencer**, *is now getting dressed.*

Thornton Bloody well stuck to you in the second half, I noticed.

Morley Aye . . . Hardly room to move about.

Thornton Was Kenny's an accident, then . . . Or someb'dy catch him?

Morley A bit slow, I think, today.

Atkinson Too cold . . .

Morley It went right through you.

Thornton There's a bloody frost out theer already . . . Shouldn't be surprised if it snows tonight . . . Jagger: grand game, lad. Well done.

Jagger Thanks, Sir Frederick.

Thornton Shook their centre a time or two, I saw.

Jagger Always goes off the bloody left foot.

Thornton So I noticed . . . (*To* **Stringer**.) Well done there, Jack. Well played.

Stringer Thanks, Sir Frederick.

Thornton One of your best games for a long time, lad . . . Not that the others haven't been so bad. (*Laughs.*) Liked your tackling. Stick to it . . . Low, low!

Stringer Aye! That's right!

Thornton Any knocks, bruises?

Stringer No. No. Be all right.

Thornton Come up tomorrow if you're feeling stiff. Lukey here'll be doing his stuff.

Luke Aye . . . That's right.

He slaps **Atkinson** *who gets up and starts to dress.*

Gi'e us a couple o' hours i' bed . . . mek it ten o'clock, old lad.

After wiping his hands **Luke** *starts to check his bottles, cotton wool, etc., packing them in his bag.*

Thornton Bloody gossip shop is this on a Sunday morning . . . Isn't that right, then, Mac?

Mackendrick Aye. It is.

Patsy I'll . . . er . . . get off, then, Sir Frederick . . . See you next week, then, all being well.

Thornton Your young lady waiting, is she?

Patsy Aye . . . I think so.

Thornton Grand game. Well done.

Patsy Thanks, Sir Frederick . . . See you next week, Mr Mackendrick.

Mackendrick Aye. Aye. Well done, young man.

Patsy Bye, lads!

Players (*without much interest*) Aye . . . bye . . . cheerio.

Morley Gi'e her a big kiss, then, Patsy, lad.

Chorus of laughter.

Jagger Gi'e her one for me, an' all.

Fenchurch And me.

Copley And me.

Fielding And me.

Atkinson And me.

Clegg And me.

Moore And me.

Spencer And me, an' all.

They laugh.

Patsy *goes: leaves through the porch entrance.*

Mackendrick Bloody good example there is Pat . . . Saves his bloody money . . . Not like some.

Clegg Saves it for bloody what, though, Mac?

Mackendrick He's got some bloody brains has Pat . . . puts it i' the bank, for one . . .

Fielding Big-headed sod.

Crosby What's that?

Luke He's got some good qualities has Pat.

Fielding I don't know where he keeps them, then.

They laugh.

Thornton (*to* **Mackendrick**) Nay, don't look at me, old lad. (*Laughs. Has gone over to the fire to warm his hands.*)

Jagger (*calling*) Sing us a song, then, Jack, old love.

Stringer Sing a bloody song thysen.

They laugh.

Owens *has come in from the office, dressed in a smart suit: a neat, cheerful, professional man.*

Owens Look at this. Bloody opening-time. Not even dressed.

Morley Where's thy been, then, Cliff?

Jagger Up in Sir Frederick's private shower-room, have you?

Owens I thought it might be crowded, lads, today. What with that and the bloody cold . . . (*Winks, crosses to the massage table. Loudly.*) Got a bit o' plaster, have you, Lukey?

Players Give over! Give over! Get off!

Owens Got a little cut here . . .

Players Give over! Give over! Get off!

Owens, *winking, goes over to the fire to warm his hands.*

Jagger Give him a bloody kiss, Sir Frederick . . . that's all he bloody wants.

They laugh.

Walsh *appears at the bath entrance, a towel around his middle. He stands in the bath entrance, nodding, looking in.*

Walsh I thought I could hear him . . . (*To* **Owens**.) Come to see the workers, have you? How long're you going to give us, lad?

Owens I'll give thee all the time thy wants, old love.

The others laugh.

Walsh (*gestures back*) I've been waiting for you, Barry . . .

The others laugh.

Fenchurch   What's thy want him for, then, Walsh?

Crosby   What's he after, Barry? What's he want?

Walsh   He knows what I've been waiting for.

They laugh.

Luke   We're bloody well closing shop in a couple o'
minutes, Walsh. You want to hurry up. You'll be turned out
without thy bloody clothes.

Atkinson   T'only bloody bath he gets is here.

They laugh. **Walsh** *still stands there, gazing in, confronted.*

Copley   Come on, then, Walshy. Show us what you've got.

Walsh   I'll show thee bloody nowt, old lad. (*Moves over
towards his clothes.*) Keeping me bloody waiting . . . sat in
theer.

They laugh.

I was *waiting* for you, Barry . . .

They laugh.

Clegg   Come on, then, Walshy, lad . . .

Fenchurch   Gi'e us a bloody shock.

Morley   Mr Mackendrick, here: he's been hanging on for
hours.

They laugh.

Mackendrick   Nay, don't bring me into it, old lad. I've
seen all of Walshy that I bloody want.

Walsh, *with great circumspection, the towel still around him, has
started to put on his clothes: vest and shirt.*

Walsh   Tell my bloody wife about you, Jagger . . . Dirty
bloody sod . . .

Crosby (*to all of them*)   Come on, come on, then. Let's have
you out . . .

Harry (*entering*)   Have you all finished, then, in theer?

Most of the players now are dressed; one or two have started to smoke. **Owens** *and* **Thornton** *stand with their backs to the fire, looking on.*

Harry *has collected up the jerseys, stockings, shorts and towels. He's worked anonymously, overlooked, almost as if, for the players, he wasn't there. Having taken out some of the boots, he comes back in.*

Walsh   What?

Harry   Have you finished with that bath?

Walsh   What do you want me to bloody do? Sup the bloody stuff, old lad?

They laugh.

Harry   I'll go and empty it, then.

Fenchurch   Mind how you touch that water, lad.

Fielding   Bloody poisonous, is that.

Harry, *without any response, goes to the hose, takes it in to the bath, reappears, turns the tap, goes off to the bath.*

Tallon *has put his head in from the office entrance. He's dressed in an overcoat and scarf, and carries a small hold-all.*

Tallon   Just say goodnight, then, lads.

Players   Aye . . . aye . . . Goodnight . . . Goodnight . . .

Tallon   A good game, lads.

Crosby   Aye.

Tallon   Both sides played very well. And in very difficult conditions, too.

Crosby   Aye. Aye. That's right.

Tallon   Sorry about Kendal . . . I hear they've taken him off.

Luke   Aye . . . He'll be all right.

Tallon   Keeping him in, then, are they?

Mackendrick   Aye. That's right.

Tallon Say goodnight, then, Mr Mackendrick . . . See you soon.

Crosses, shakes hands with **Mackendrick**.

Mackendrick I don't think you've met Sir Frederick.

Tallon No. No. I haven't.

Thornton Admired your refereeing very much.

Tallon Thank you. Thank you very much, sir.

Thornton See you up here again, then, soon, I hope.

Tallon Aye. Aye. Our job, though, you never know.

Thornton If you bring the same result with you, you can come up every bloody week, tha knows.

They laugh.

Going upstairs, then, are you? (*Mimes drink.*)

Tallon No. No. I've to catch me train. Otherwise I would. This weather. You can never chance your luck . . . Well, goodbye. It's been a pleasure.

Nods to **Owens**, *ducks his head to the others, goes.*

Walsh Anybody heard the bloody two-thirty?

Jagger No.

Fenchurch No.

Spencer No.

Luke No.

Fielding No.

Moore No.

Walsh (*back to them, getting dressed*) By God, sunk me bloody week's wages theer . . . You haven't got a paper, Mac?

Mackendrick No. No. Haven't had a chance.

Copley Let's see. Now here's one . . . What wa're it, now?

Walsh (*dressing*) Two-thirty.

Copley (*reading*) 'One o'clock . . . one-thirty . . . two o'clock . . . two-fifteen . . .'

Walsh Come on, come on, come on . . .

Jagger *points it out.*

Copley Two-thirty! . . . Let's see now. What d'thy bet?

Walsh Just tell us the bloody winner. Come on. Come on.

Copley What's this, now? . . . Can't see without me glasses . . . Little . . . what is it?

Walsh Oh, God.

Copley Nell.

Walsh Hell fire . . . Can't bloody well go home tonight.

Copley (*still reading*) Worth having something on, was that.

Walsh Tell bloody Jagger: don't tell me.

Jagger And Fenny. (*Winking.*)

Walsh And Fenny . . . Here. Let's have a look.

They wait, watching, suppressing their laughter as **Walsh**, *eyes screwed up, shortsighted, reads.*

Here! . . . Here! . . . What's this . . . (*Eyes screwed, still reads.*)

They burst out laughing.

Just look at that. Bloody Albatross! *Seven to one!*

Shows it to **Atkinson** *to be confirmed.*

Atkinson That's right.

Walsh I've won, I've won.

Embraces **Stringer**, *who's standing near him, fastening his coat.*

Stringer Go on. Go on. Ger off!

The players laugh.

Walsh By God. That's made my bloody day, has that.

Mackendrick More interested in that than he is in bloody football.

Walsh I am. I am, old lad . . . More bloody brass in this for a bloody start. (*Laughs, finishes his dressing.*) By God, then: see old Barry now . . . Wish thy'd washed my bloody back, then, don't you?

Copley I think I bloody do. That's right.

They laugh.

Fielding Well, then, lads. I'm off . . .

Players See you, Fieldy . . . Bye.

Luke Watch that bloody eye.

Fielding Aye. Aye. It'll be all right.

Thornton Bye, Fieldy. Well done, lad.

Fielding Aye . . . (*Goes.*)

Jagger Fenny . . . Ar' t'a barn, then? . . . Trev?

Fenchurch (*packing his bag*) Aye . . .

Trevor Aye.

Walsh Lukey . . . where's my bloody cigar, old lad!

They laugh. **Luke** *gets out the cigar.*

Jagger *and* **Trevor** *have gone to the door. They're joined by* **Fenchurch** *carrying his bag.*

Jagger See you, lads, then.

All Aye.

Trevor Bye.

All Bye . . . See you.

Mackendrick Well done, Trevor, lad.

Trevor Aye . . .

They go.

Walsh *is lighting up.*

Thornton (*going*) Mind you don't choke on that, then, Walshy.

Walsh Don't bloody worry . . . From now on . . . Trouble free! (*Blows out a cloud of smoke for his amusement.*)

Thornton Bye, lads . . . Clifford?

Owens Aye. Shan't be a minute.

Thornton Time for a snifter, lads, tha knows . . . (*Gestures up.*)

All Aye . . .

Copley Bye, Sir Frederick . . .

Thornton *goes through the office entrance.* **Mackendrick,** *nodding, follows.*

Crosby, *picking up a couple of remaining boots, goes off through the bath entrance.*

Stringer Well, I've got everything, I think. I'm off.

Copley Enjoyed yourself today, then, Jack?

Stringer Aye. All right.

Clegg They tell me your mother was here this afternoon, then, Jack.

Stringer As likely.

Copley T'only bloody fan he's got.

Stringer I've got one or two more, an' all.

They laugh.

Atkinson Give you a lift into town, Jack, if you like.

Stringer No . . . no . . . I like to walk. (*He goes.*)

They laugh.

Walsh Here . . . Here you are, then, Cliff.

Walsh, *having finished dressing, adjusted his buttonhole and combed his hair in the mirror, gets out another cigar. The others watch in amazement.*

Owens   Thanks, Walshy . . . Thanks very much . . . Won't smoke it now. (*Smells it appreciatively.*)

Walsh   Save it.

Owens   Appreciate it later.

Walsh   Not like these ignorant bloody sods . . .

Copley   Well, bloody hell . . .

Walsh   Come today, tha knows . . . All gone tomorrer.

Clegg   Bloody hell.

Copley   The stingy bugger . . .

Walsh *laughs: a last look round: coat.*

Crosby *comes back in through bath entrance.*

Crosby   Come on. Come on. Let's have you out. (*Claps his hands.*)

Clegg   A bloody fistful . . .

Walsh   Just one. Just one. (*Puffs at his own.*) Just the odd one, old son.

Copley   Greasing round the bloody captain, Danny.

Walsh   Keep in wi' me bloody captain. Never know when you might need a bloody favour. Isn't that right, then, Cliff?

Owens   That's right.

They laugh, going.

Atkinson   Well, then, Walshy . . . (*Gestures up.*) Gonna buy us one?

Walsh   I might . . .

They've moved over to the office door, except for **Owens, Crosby** *and* **Luke**.

Moore *stands to one side.*

Barry here, o' course, will have to do without . . . (*To* **Crosby**.) Never came when I bloody called . . . As for the rest . . . I might stand a round . . . Might afford it . . . And one for thee, old lad. All right?

Spencer   All right.

Walsh (*looking back*)   What was Jagger's horse, now?

Luke   Little Nell.

Walsh   Little Nell! (*He laughs.*)

Clegg   Are you coming, Frank?

Moore   Aye. Aye. I will.

Walsh (*to* **Moore**)   Thy's kept bloody quiet, old lad . . .

Moore   Aye . . .

Walsh   Don't let these bloody lads upset you.

Moore   No. No. (*Laughs.*)

Walsh (*puts his arm round* **Moore**'s *shoulder, going*)   Sithee, Barry . . . first flush o' bloody success is that.

Copley (*leaving*)   Mic?

Morley   Aye. Just about.

They go, laughing. Burst of laughter and shouts outside.

Silence. **Luke** *has packed his bag; he zips it up.* **Crosby** *is picking up the rest of the equipment: odd socks, shirts.*

Owens *gets out a cigarette; offers one to* **Crosby** *who takes one, then offers one to* **Luke** *who shakes his head.*

There's a sound of **Harry** *singing off: hymn.*

Owens *flicks a lighter. Lights* **Crosby**'s *cigarette, then his own.*

Crosby   Not two bloody thoughts to rub together . . . (*Gestures off.*) Walshy.

Owens   No. (*Laughs.*)

Crosby   Years ago . . . ran into a bloody post . . . out yonder . . . split the head of any other man . . . Gets up:

looks round: says, 'By God', then . . . 'Have they teken him off?'

They laugh. **Luke** *swings down his bag.*

Luke I'm off.

Crosby See you, Lukey.

Luke Cliff . . .

Owens Thanks, Lukey.

Luke (*calls*) Bye, Harry . . .

They wait. Hymn continues.

Crosby Wandered off . . . (*Taps his head: indicates* **Harry** *off.*)

Luke Aye . . . See you, lads. (*Collects autograph books.*)

Owens Bye, Lukey.

Luke *goes with his bag through the porch entrance.*

Crosby *picks up the last pieces. Hymn finishes.*

Crosby How're you feeling?

Owens Stiff.

Crosby Bloody past it, lad, tha knows.

Owens Aye. One more season, I think: I'm finished.

Crosby *laughs.*

Been here, tha knows, a bit too long.

Crosby Nay, there's nob'dy else, old lad . . .

Owens Aye . . . (*Laughs.*)

Crosby Need thee a bit longer to keep these lads in line.

Owens Aye. (*Laughs.*)

Crosby Did well today.

Owens They did. That's right.

Crosby Bloody leadership, tha see, that counts.

Owens (*laughs*) Aye . . .

Crosby (*calls through to bath*)   Have you finished, then, in theer . . .

No answer.

(*To* **Owens**.) Ger up yonder . . .

Owens   Have a snifter . . .

Crosby   Another bloody season yet.

Puts out the light.

Poor old Fieldy.

Owens   Aye.

Crosby   Ah, well . . . this time tomorrer.

Owens   Have no more bloody worries then.

They laugh. **Crosby** *puts his arm round* **Owens**. *They go. Pause.*

Harry *comes in, looks round. He carries a sweeping brush. Starts sweeping. Picks up one or two bits of tape, etc. Turns on the Tannoy: light music.*

Sweeps.

The remaining light and the sound of the Tannoy slowly fade.

Curtain.

Cromwell

Characters

Logan
O'Halloran
Morgan
Proctor
Chamberlain
Moore
Mathew
Margaret
Joan
Kennedy
Broome
Cleet
Wallace
Drake
Boatman
First Soldier
Second Soldier
First Traveller
Second Traveller
Third Traveller
Crowd

Cromwell was first presented at the Royal Court Theatre, London, on 15 August 1973, with the following cast:

Logan	Jarlath Conroy
O'Halloran	Albert Finney
Morgan	Alun Armstrong
Proctor	Brian Cox
Chamberlain	Colin Douglas
Moore	John Barrett
Mathew	Mark McManus
Margaret	Anne Dyson
Joan	Frances Tomelty
Kennedy	Martin Read
Broome	Peter Postlethwaite
Cleet	Kenneth Colley
Wallace	Alun Armstrong
Drake	Colin Bennett
Boatman	Colin Douglas
Soldiers	Conrad Asquith
	Forbes Collins
	Alan Ford
	Mike Melia
Travellers	John Barrett
	Anne Dyson
	Alan Ford
	Mike Melia
	Diana Rayworth

Directed by Anthony Page
Designed by Jocelyn Herbert

Act One

Scene One

A stage. **Logan** *enters, rubbing his hands: Irish, in his thirties.*

Logan   Don't they ever heat this place?

He's followed in by **O'Halloran**, *also Irish.*

O'Halloran   Not if they can help it ... Anybody up there, is there?

Logan (*gazing*)   No. No. Not a thing. (*Calls.*) Anybody up there, is there?

Pause.

O'Halloran   No answer.

Logan   Nothing.

O'Halloran   Not a person.

Logan   Jesus, but it's bloody cold.

O'Halloran   Here ... here! Go on, then. Have a tap! (*Holds up flat of his hand: they start sparring.*)

Morgan *comes in.*

Morgan   Always fighting.

Logan   What?

O'Halloran   What's that?

Logan   Fight you, young man, if you don't watch out.

Morgan   One hand behind my back, or both?

Logan   You or me, O'Halloran?

O'Halloran   No, no. Age before beauty, Patrick, every time.

Morgan   Go on, go on. (*Holds chin out.*)

Logan   Ah, now, er . . . a little to the left . . . No, no.
The right.

O'Halloran   More in the middle.

Logan   More in the middle, now . . . that's right.

Morgan *has swivelled his chin from left to right: now holds it up
even more invitingly.*

Logan   Right hand, now, or left . . . Should get us warm
this, Stephen.

O'Halloran   Oh, undoubtedly . . .

Logan   Should I falter . . .

O'Halloran   Could always carry on.

Logan   That's right.

O'Halloran   Ready, Morgan, are you?

Morgan   Ready? I've been ready half an hour.

Logan   Upper cut or overarm, O'Halloran?

O'Halloran   Oh, overarm! . . . Then, again: the uppercut
has a great deal to recommend it.

Logan   I think you're right . . . the short left jab has
always been my favourite.

O'Halloran   More a defensive blow, I thought.

Logan   More a defensive blow: you're right.

O'Halloran   Left hook, now, is a different matter.

Logan   Left hook, you know: I think you're right.

O'Halloran   Or the old one-two.

Logan   Ah, God.

O'Halloran   Shan't see its like.

Logan   No, no . . .

Morgan   Are you going to take a swipe, or aren't you?

Logan   Steady on, now, Morgan.

O'Halloran   Doesn't he know we've got all day?

Morgan   All day for talking . . .

O'Halloran   Talking?

Logan   Talking?

O'Halloran   Isn't he aware . . .

Logan   That there's a great distinction . . .

O'Halloran   Between talking . . .

Logan   And discussion.

Morgan   Have you got the guts to have a swipe? (*Holds out chin.*) Go on. Go on . . . Left hand or right.

Logan   There: there, now. If I hit him as hard as I can . . . (*Looks round.*) There's bound to be inquiries.

Morgan   I think you're suffering from one or two delusions, Logan, if you don't mind my saying so.

Logan   Oh yes.

Morgan   Not least, that you've got the courage to hit me on the jaw at all.

Logan   I've got the courage, right enough.

O'Halloran   And the strength.

Logan   And the strength . . . What I've got a superabundance of as well . . .

Morgan   Oh, yes?

Logan *looks to* **O'Halloran**. *Then:*

O'Halloran   Compassion.

Logan   Compassion.

O'Halloran   Compassion, there: I think you're right.

Morgan   I'm not standing here, you know, all morning.

Logan That's what the English lack.

O'Halloran They do.

Logan Amongst many other things.

Morgan What's that?

Logan Ah, now: I don't think it'd be safe to mention it.

O'Halloran No, no: I think you're right.

Morgan I'm Welsh.

O'Halloran and **Logan** *exchange looks. Silent: they sit, lean back; lounge.*

Logan Oh, it's a great morning. (*Stretching.*)

O'Halloran A great morning, Patrick, surely . . . (*Yawns, stretches.*) A great morning, there . . . I think you're right.

Light fades.

Scene Two

Light comes up.

Logan and **O'Halloran** *are lying on the ground;* **Morgan** *is sitting, straw in mouth.*

Proctor *comes in.*

Proctor Anybody here, then?

O'Halloran No, no . . . deserted.

Proctor By God: they tell you get here early . . . you come on time: no one has arrived.

Proctor *looks around: stretches: crouches down.*

Logan They say the feller himself is due past any time.

Proctor You seen him, Mr Logan, have you?

Logan No, no. I never have.

Proctor *looks to* **O'Halloran**.

O'Halloran   No. No. Me neither.

Logan   Mr Morgan?

Morgan   No ... No.

O'Halloran   They say he has an arm ...

Morgan   Yes?

O'Halloran   Twice as thick as his leg.

Logan   Is that a fact?

O'Halloran   And hair ...

Logan   Yes?

O'Halloran   I better not describe it.

Logan   Oh, now ...

O'Halloran   As rough as a witch's broom.

Logan   To God.

O'Halloran   Can sweep a room ...

Logan   No. No. You're telling me ...

O'Halloran   As easy as a glance.

Logan *looks to the others, seemingly amazed.*

Proctor   I saw him once.

Logan   Is that a fact?

Morgan   Is he like O'Halloran says?

Proctor   I saw him in the wood ... passing between the trees ... a kind of ...

O'Halloran   Mist.

Proctor   That's right ...

O'Halloran   They say, from a distance – because they'll never let you close – he looks rather like, shall we say ...

Logan   A moving vapour.

Proctor   It's always misty in the woods . . .

O'Halloran   People passing by . . .

Logan   Assume something of the same condition.

O'Halloran (*about to add something else – then:*)   That's right.

Logan *whistles a tune: cheerful, perky. Then:*

Morgan   We could build a fire.

O'Halloran   What's that?

Morgan   Wood . . . There's plenty lying about.

O'Halloran   But then . . .

Logan   We mightn't be here for very long.

O'Halloran   No sooner has the wood been laid.

Logan   Than along he comes . . .

O'Halloran   'And you . . . And you . . . And you,' he says . . .

Logan   Up on your feet . . .

O'Halloran   And off.

Logan   And all that wood'll go to waste.

O'Halloran   And all the effort with it.

Proctor   It's certainly cold. (*Rubbing his hands, he starts to pace.*) Whatever he says . . . we can't sit here for long.

Light slowly fades.

Scene Three

Light comes up.

The men are sitting or lying, silent.

Chamberlain *comes in, a well-built, sturdy, middle-aged man.*

Chamberlain Are these, then, the only ones who came?

Morgan We're the only bloody ones who have.

Proctor Do you know where we have to go?

Chamberlain I do.

O'Halloran Come on, then, for God's sake . . . sitting here . . .

Chamberlain You should have been there some time ago.

Logan We've been sitting here . . .

O'Halloran We have.

Logan For hours.

O'Halloran Just look at me bloody fingers . . .

Logan Dropping off.

O'Halloran Not fit to do a job, we're not.

Logan God: feet likewise. Can hardly stand.

Proctor How far do we have to go?

Chamberlain Not far.

Morgan Walking, is it? Or do we have a ride?

Chamberlain Walking. Unless you've something of your own.

Morgan No. No.

Logan No, no.

O'Halloran Too bloody poor.

Logan Too bloody poor. That's right.

O'Halloran Not find a cart, nor animal . . . nor anything on four legs round here.

Morgan I'm surprised . . .

Logan Your honour . . .

Chamberlain   Chamberlain.

Morgan   Mr Chamberlain, sir, I'm surprised you've not got a conveyance of your own.

Chamberlain   I had. It was shot away . . . There's been fighting in the woods all day. I'm surprised you haven't heard.

O'Halloran   We have.

Chamberlain   You did nothing, then, but sit in here.

Logan   Can't fight armed men, you know, with sticks.

Chamberlain   Some people, I'll have you know, have fought with less . . . By the time the sun has set it might be you.

Logan   To God.

O'Halloran   Come on, for God's sake, then: get off.

Chamberlain   There was no one in the village but women and children as I was passing through.

Proctor   They've all run off.

Logan   Except for one or two.

Proctor   Except for us.

Logan   Damn fine fools we were, I'm thinking.

Morgan   We were.

Logan   To think of even coming here at all.

Proctor   Somebody has to stay and fight.

Morgan   Somebody it could have been: not us.

Chamberlain   What's your name, then?

Proctor   Proctor.

Chamberlain   Do you have a job?

Proctor   I had . . . After today, I'm not so sure.

Chamberlain *looks to* **Morgan**.

Morgan   A dairy ... That's to say, two weeks ago I had a cow.

Logan   Labourer.

O'Halloran   Labourer.

Logan   The common kind ...

O'Halloran   The common kind.

Logan   Itinerant.

O'Halloran   Itinerant! The very word.

Logan   The very phrase I had in mind.

O'Halloran *and* **Logan** *laugh*.

Proctor   I had a smithy: no metal things to mend.

Chamberlain   No weapons, then?

Proctór   No, no. Ploughs there were: a harness, scythes; a metal gate or two.

Chamberlain   I'm surprised you haven't a horse.

Proctor   I had: went the same way as Morgan's cow.

O'Halloran   They're eating rats, you know, round here ...

Logan   Grass, leaves ...

O'Halloran   Even, they tell me, a corpse or two ...

Logan   Fresh killed.

O'Halloran   Fresh killed.

Logan   Or not so fresh.

O'Halloran   Or not so fresh. I think he's right.

Proctor (*to* **Chamberlain**)   Will we be fed do you think tonight?

No answer: **Chamberlain** *is looking off, preparatory to leaving.*

Will we be fed, do you think, sir, when we reach this place
tonight?

Chamberlain   We might ... I'm hoping so. (*Looks round:
sees them watching him – then:*) If we set off now. I think we
might.

Morgan   Are you walking, then, like us?

Chamberlain   I have no choice.

O'Halloran   Did the feller send for us himself?

Chamberlain   All able-bodied men ... That's right.

Logan   Then that lets you and me out, O'Halloran, for a
bloody start.

They laugh.

Not have to carry you or something? On the back.

Chamberlain   No, no. I'll walk along. Just like
yourselves.

O'Halloran   To God, now ... but that's a bloody
sight ...

Logan   One sent by himself ...

O'Halloran   Walking on the track.

Logan   Two feet.

O'Halloran   Two feet.

Logan   And two beautiful, fine, long legs to match.

Logan *and* **O'Halloran** *laugh.*

Chamberlain   Are you ready, then? We've waited here
too long already.

Proctor   Aye ... There's nothing now to keep us here.

Chamberlain   We'll skirt the woods ... you can show
the way.

O'Halloran *starts back.*

Chamberlain   Since you know the place so well, that is.

They begin to leave.

Light fades.

Scene Four

Light comes up.

The light comes up on a wooden coffin lying on a cart. There's the distant roar of cannon.

O'Halloran *has come in.*

O'Halloran   Jesus now: but there's a rare old sight.

Logan (*following him in*)   Food at last . . .

O'Halloran   Cooked, do you think . . .

Logan   Waitin' to be served.

O'Halloran   Undoubtedly someone special.

Logan   Somebody very grand!

Proctor (*coming in*)   That's the first we've seen inside a box.

Logan   The lid's been fastened down. (*Trying it.*)

O'Halloran (*looks round*)   Could hardly have done the thing himself.

Logan   No, no. I'd say that someone's done it for him . . . Pinned down, he is.

O'Halloran   Oh, snug and cosy.

Logan   A cart to ride upon, at that.

O'Halloran (*as* **Chamberlain** *enters, tiredly*)   Jesus: but that noise is getting close.

Logan   Either that . . .

O'Halloran   Or my bloody stomach . . .

Logan   Is grumbling here from lack of food.

Chamberlain *looks round.*

Chamberlain   Was this standing here, then, unattended?

Logan   Aye. It was, it was . . . quite on its own. No one to trouble . . .

O'Halloran   . . . or protect it.

Morgan (*coming in last, weary*)   Have you tried the lid?

O'Halloran   He has.

Proctor   It's nothing of our concern . . . We better leave it.

Logan   To God, now, man . . . And what about the cart?

Chamberlain   The one goes with the other, I would have thought.

O'Halloran   The one goes with us, I would have thought, might sound a little better.

O'Halloran *joins* **Logan** *to try the coffin.*

There, now, but that's a weight.

Logan   More like two or three, I would have thought, inside.

O'Halloran   Proctor: aren't you going to give a soul a hand.

Proctor   I've seen enough of the dead and dying . . . I've seen enough for all my life: I'm damned if I want to touch one that's decently encased. Cart or no cart. You can shift the thing yourself.

O'Halloran   Morgan . . . you Welshy bastard, aren't you going to give a lift?

Logan   And who's to push the bleeding thing: that's what I would like to ask.

O'Halloran   We'll take it turn and turn about.

Logan Aye? And who's to ride on first?

Logan The stringy bastard: I'll lift the thing myself. (*Hoists up one end of the coffin.*)

Moore *comes on: an old man.*

Moore Would you leave that ... Would you leave it, sir?

O'Halloran To God. And who the hell is this?

Moore I'm the brother of the one inside ... and the cart, like the corpse, your honour, is part of mine.

Logan I'll be damned: but the shape you're in you ought to be in there with him.

O'Halloran Have you pushed the thing yourself?

Morgan I have ... with a little help.

Logan Not from up above, I'm thinking.

Moore No, no ... I have a friend.

Mathew *has come on: a sinewy, ragged, frantic creature.*

O'Halloran In the same condition as yourself.

Moore We haven't eaten for a day ... And the day before was hardly better ... if we've anything to take, then take it ... But not the cart.

Logan Bejasus: it's not the box we're after.

Mathew *has started making signs.*

Moore He doesn't speak.

Morgan From choice, you mean.

Proctor No, no, you see ...

Chamberlain The man's afflicted.

Logan To God: he'll defend it with his life! (*Laughs at* **Mathew**'s *wild gestures.*) Go on! Go on! Go on there, now! (*Makes gestures to provoke him.*)

O'Halloran One old man, a fool: why don't we bury

the thing, and take the cart.

Logan   Aye. Aye. We'll dispose of the one . . .

O'Halloran   And take care of the other.

Logan (*to* **Moore**)   For after that . . .

O'Halloran   There'll be no need . . .

Logan   For either of you to want it longer.

Margaret *has come in: a middle-aged woman.*

Margaret   The body cannot be buried here . . . Nor anywhere but on consecrated ground.

O'Halloran   Jasus: but how many more have we got to come?

Logan   Hiding, are you, in the trees? (*Looking off.*)

Margaret   There's no one else.

Moore   This is my niece . . . my brother's only child.

O'Halloran   More beautiful, I would imagine, than the one inside.

He and **Logan** *laugh.*

Morgan *has collapsed on the ground, resting.*

Proctor, *having already set off, waits now, gazing back.*

Chamberlain, *though taking in the situation, still watches off.*

Morgan   It's the cart they're after, not your father, girl.

Proctor (*reapproaching*)   If he was so precious, why did you leave him here like this?

Margaret   We thought it was the soldiers . . .

Moore   Coming through the wood.

Mathew *gestures off.*

O'Halloran   Aye. Soldiers we are, I hope, in a couple of hours.

Morgan Aye. With a soldier's pay, and a soldier's grub.

Logan Which is not a sentiment, madam, that I share myself.

Proctor There's a church we passed, an hour ago, a priest . . . why don't you take him there?

Moore That's not a Roman church, you see.

O'Halloran Are you one of us?

Margaret We are . . . (*She looks from one to the other.*) It seems we are.

Logan And look at this.

O'Halloran Not one more left.

Morgan Then where's she from?

Joan *has come in: a girl, nineteen or twenty.*

Joan I couldn't wait there any longer. If they're one of us then we've nothing to fear.

Morgan *has half got up, rising to his knees.*

O'Halloran How many more have you got back there?

Logan Is this the first of a regular troupe?

Moore These people are under my protection.

Margaret This is my daughter: there's no one else.

Joan The road's safe, then: these men – they'll let us pass?

O'Halloran Aye, now . . . aren't we going the same way, too? . . . The cart, if I'm not mistaken, is pointing in the same direction.

Chamberlain We've not time to wait with these: it's getting late . . . The sun's down now to the tops of the trees.

Logan And which way do we go from here. . . ?

Chamberlain I thought you knew the route.

Logan I do . . .

O'Halloran But not the one, you see, we've taken . . . (*To* **Moore**, *by whom he's come to stand.*) You see, we've been so much hedged about . . . cutting this way, cutting that . . . avoiding the armies moving in the woods . . . that by now we're miles from the road we took. (*Looks about him, head raised.*) You couldn't show us the way, old man, yourself.

Moore We've been travelling as it is for several days . . .

Logan But that's the smell . . . It's pouring from the box! (*Moves back.*) Good God . . . Infection, man, you see. Look out!

Moore My niece can't let her father rest without the last rites being passed above his head.

Margaret Our own priest left.

Moore He'd been hiding in the woods for days.

Margaret The soldiers came.

Joan They searched the farm . . .

Margaret Fortunately, by then, that night, my father died . . . (*To* **O'Halloran**.) Since then, you see, we've travelled with the cart.

Logan But then, if the man is one of us . . .

O'Halloran Aren't we moving generally – hopefully, ma'am, I might even say – in the same direction?

Logan A young lady like yourself.

O'Halloran Without protection . . .

Logan But for an old man, an idiot . . . and an ageing wife.

O'Halloran (*to* **Margaret**) Your husband, I take it, has been captured like ourselves . . . enlisted in the war.

Margaret He has . . .

Joan He volunteered.

Margaret It was something he believed in.

Joan And now he's dead.

O'Halloran Fatherless as well, to boot ... Morgan ... Get up on your feet, there, man ... Logan: take this side ... and you take this.

Morgan And what are you going to do, O'Halloran, yourself?

O'Halloran I shall direct the cart, and watch the track ... avoid the bog-holes, and watch the trees around ... Proctor? Are you going to lend a hand?

Proctor Aye. I suppose there's nothing left to lose ... (*To* **Chamberlain**.) If he's lost the way he'll not direct us back.

Logan Are you coming, Mr Chamberlain? Or will you find your own way on from here?

Chamberlain Aye ... (*He looks about.*) It's too late now to search round for a track ... (*He lifts his head at the sound of guns.*) In any case, when we get there, I've a feeling it's going to be too late.

The men have lifted the cart: they set it to the track.

O'Halloran Would a fair hand like yours do you think be strong enough to help me with the tiller.

Joan Yes. I'll help.

Margaret I'll help as well.

O'Halloran No, no, now, lady: you've pushed enough. You walk on with the gentlemen behind ...

Mathew *has already gripped the side of the cart to push.*

O'Halloran (*to* **Joan**) I think, between ourselves, with the help we have in hand, we'll manage ... Are you ready, fellers, then? ... And ... heave!

They move off.

Light fades.

Scene Five

Light comes up.

O'Halloran *and* **Joan** *sit on the ground: half-light, and flickering light, off, from a fire.*

Behind them, some distance off, **Mathew** *moves up and down, gesturing, restless, as if talking to them, or with himself.*

O'Halloran   What sort of farm did you have?

Joan   Oh ... crops ...

O'Halloran   Cattle?

Joan   We had a few ...

O'Halloran   I'm a great cattle man, of course, myself.

Joan   Yes?

O'Halloran   There's not many a thing I don't know about cows ... As for beef and bulls ... There's many a man I've never set eyes on come asking for advice.

Joan   When the soldiers came they drove them off.

O'Halloran (*watches her. Then:*) You'll go back there when the old man's safe beneath the ground?

Joan   I might.

O'Halloran   What other places are there, then?

Joan   I've only known the farm. I couldn't tell.

O'Halloran   I've travelled far and wide, meself.

She doesn't answer.

Do I look a travelled man, d'you think?

Joan   I don't know ... You look like any other.

O'Halloran   Lines of experience ... If the light was a little stronger you could trace them out ... There ... (*Takes her hand: puts it to his face.*) ... Eyes and cheek ... And particularly around the mouth.

Mathew *has come closer, gesturing, miming speech.*

O'Halloran   God: that smell is strong ... Wouldn't it be better to bury him, do you think?

Joan   It depends how strong you feel.

O'Halloran   I feel strong enough ... I feel strong enough to put him in the ground meself.

Joan   My mother can't ... Without a blessing ... Even if there's nothing left but bone: without that he'll find no rest. And without that, *she*'ll find none either.

O'Halloran   Superstition ... I'd bury the man myself: put damn stones inside the box ... She'd never know ... And *he*'s too far gone, I think, to bother much himself ... There's nothing beyond death, you know.

Joan *doesn't answer.*

O'Halloran   And what is there, then, that you could put your finger on right now?

She shakes her head.

There's the stars up yonder, there's the two of us down here ... between the three – them, us and it (*Indicating coffin.*) – can you see anything else intruding? ... Not counting that raving lunatic o' course.

Pause.

Joan   When the soldiers came, the day he died, I saw them first about a mile away ... on horses ... they came over to the field at the back of the house: it was full of crops: potatoes mainly ...

O'Halloran   I've seen them across that sort of space myself ... Damn great fellers: like trees, they are ... I've often thought I'd make a damn fine soldier boy meself ...

tall, handsome . . . a commanding presence . . . if I could
only keep my backside on top of a horse I'd have been
one of the King's men, I'm thinking, long ago . . . I've
often wondered . . .

Joan *looks across at him.*

O'Halloran How I've eluded conscription by the army-
men so long . . . a natural gift like mine . . . you'd imagine
they'd have put it to some militaristic use, now, long ago
. . . Ah, well . . . it needs an eye to spot an eye . . . and if
the eyes on one side, you know, are not so good . . . then
ones like mine go unattended.

Joan I've seen one die.

O'Halloran What? (*He looks behind him.*)

Joan The day they came I found one lying in the hedge
. . . he'd got a pipe . . . It was the smoke I saw at first . . .
rising . . . a thin blue cloud . . . it settled round the twigs
and leaves . . . 'There's a fire over there,' I thought . . .
when I went across I saw a boot . . . It was sticking out . . .
It had a hole, the size of this . . . in the middle of the sole
. . . and when I looked between the leaves I saw an eye . . .

O'Halloran To God. (*He glances up, behind, at the now still
and listening* **Mathew**.)

Joan At first, I thought he'd been asleep . . . eyes open,
now, the pipe still in his hand . . . When I got up close . . .

O'Halloran Go on, go on.

Joan I saw his throat.

O'Halloran To God . . .

Joan From ear to ear.

O'Halloran Is that a fact?

Joan The ash had fallen from his pipe . . . and started
smouldering in the grass . . .

O'Halloran Just sitting there: to have a rest. Got out his pipe ... (*Looks behind:* **Mathew** *stands gazing over.*) What happened then?

Joan I saw the soldiers ... riding to the field ... When they came up close I ran back to the house: they were looking at the crops.

O'Halloran For food.

Joan Or him ... I warned them at the house, and when I came back out, they were riding by the hedge.

O'Halloran Go on. Go on ...

Joan I thought we'd be taken then for sure ... a soldier murdered ... almost at the door ... They rode straight past: came right into the yard ... looking at the spot it seemed itself.

O'Halloran Go on, then, girl. What happened next?

Joan They asked what crops we had. They looked inside the house, the barn ... an hour later, when they left, we ran down to the hedge ... (*Looks up at* **O'Halloran**.) The grass was flattened. Nothing else. A smudge of ash where the pipe had been.

O'Halloran Don't tell me he'd got up and walked away himself.

Joan I've no idea.

O'Halloran (*looks round him once again*) They're mystical fellers ... I'll grant you that.

Joan The soldiers came back an hour later ... By then, my grandfather had been fastened in his coffin ... It would have broken his heart to see the things they took ... The cattle ... They dug the fields ... took all the roots ... there was nothing left ... That night we set off for a priest ... and found he'd fled ... We've been walking ever since ... A week: it must be more ... At first we had some food ... and then ... everywhere we went burnt fields, houses, even churches left in ruins ...

Chamberlain *passes across the back.*

Chamberlain   I'll put the fire down . . . As bright as that we'll soon be seen.

Joan   Who is he? Is he one of you?

O'Halloran   He's the recruiting sergeant, so to speak . . . The gentleman who wants to enlist us in his troop sent him off to pick us up, and one or two others who, in the circumstances, thought it discreeter to go wandering in the woods . . . His horse got shot away: he escaped himself and, so to speak, lost us as well . . . And what do you call the lunatic jumper, then? (*Indicating* **Mathew**.)

Joan   That's Mathew . . . He's been with my father all his life.

O'Halloran   And you yourself?

Joan   I'm Joan.

O'Halloran   That's a hard, reliable name . . . Mine's O'Halloran . . . Stephen to my friends . . . Your mother's name: I thought I heard it as we came along?

Joan   Margaret.

O'Halloran   If that isn't just as fine a name as well.

Chamberlain *has come back.*

Chamberlain   I think the firing's dying down.

O'Halloran   Either that, or we're going deaf from lack of food.

Chamberlain   When the sun's up we'll find the road. (*To* **Joan**.) I'm afraid we'll have to leave you then.

O'Halloran   Ah, to God, your honour: they can go with us.

Chamberlain   Only if our ways combine: their way with ours . . . I'll leave you, then . . . Keep your voices down . . . (*Goes.*)

O'Halloran Don't worry ... No need any more, I think, for words ...

Light fades.

Scene Six

The light comes up on the cart: pushed by **Morgan**, **Proctor** *and* **Mathew**.

O'Halloran *has come on ahead: pauses. He holds up his hand to halt.*

O'Halloran Jesus, now: but there's someone there ...

Logan, *holding a rope fastened to the cart, comes on behind.*

Proctor I've heard no firing now for hours.

Logan The battle's over: I think we've won.

Chamberlain (*coming on*) Are you lost again ...

O'Halloran No, no. There's someone there.

Margaret *has come on immediately behind the cart: she's followed by* **Moore** *who has to be helped by* **Joan**. **Margaret** *goes back to draw him on.*

Chamberlain I can't see anything but the bloody wood.

Logan His temper shortens by the hour.

O'Halloran It does.

Logan God: but we'll have a rest at least. (*Sinks down.*)

Morgan *sinks down too.*

Proctor He's right, you know. There's someone there.

Logan Go on: go on. I'll have a look. (*Looks round: otherwise he makes no gesture.*)

Moore (*coming further on now, with* **Margaret**'s *and* **Joan**'s *help*) Are we lost again? Or do the paths divide?

Joan There's someone in the wood ahead.

Morgan They've marvellous eyes: I can't see a bloody thing meself . . .

Chamberlain It's nothing but the light . . . Let's push ahead.

Logan You go yourself: I'm sittin' here.

Margaret If there's someone there, why aren't they coming out?

O'Halloran They're watching us . . .

Proctor They're making sure . . .

Logan They're counting up and then . . . they'll pounce.

Proctor There's one of them . . . He's over there. (*Points off diagonally behind.*)

Logan Good God: we're bloody done for now.

Morgan Why don't we run while we have a chance?

O'Halloran There's another over there . . .

Logan And there.

Morgan I told you we shouldn't have stayed with these . . .

Proctor Too late to run: they're all around.

Logan There's another one, you see – ahead.

They draw together. **Kennedy**, *a soldier, comes on. He walks slowly round.*

Kennedy What's this?

O'Halloran A box.

Kennedy And what's inside?

Logan Come nearer and you'll begin to smell.

Moore It's the body of my brother.

Margaret   We're taking it to a place of rest.

Kennedy   And who are these?

Moore   This is my brother's grandchild . . . and this his daughter.

Broome, *a second soldier, comes on.*

Kennedy   And him? (*Indicating* **Mathew**.)

Moore   A servant of the house.

Broome   And these?

Joan   These are men from the village, who came to help.

Broome   Five men: one cart?

Pause.

Kennedy   What denomination are you, then?

O'Halloran   Protestant.

Logan   Oh, Protestant.

Kennedy   I've never heard of a Protestant before . . .

Broome   Speaking with a Celtic tongue.

O'Halloran   Oh, thousands, thousands: all around.

Broome   And you?

Chamberlain   I'm one of these.

Broome   Five men to pull one cart.

O'Halloran   All volunteers.

Broome   That's what I thought . . . (*Examines cart: lifts handle. To* **Moore**.) An older, or a younger brother, then?

Moore   Older . . . Much older.

Broome   And much lighter than yourself.

Moore   He was.

Broome   And yet the weight in here is like a ton of lead.

Margaret   I've never felt the weight myself.

Broome   Have you never touched the box?

Margaret   Not since I saw him put inside.

Broome   I think we'll have the lid up, then.

Margaret   No!

Joan   Never.

Broome   We've seen this artifice before ... A man brought through our lines, with more than a thousand pounds upon his head.

Logan   To God ... Is this what we've been let in for, then.

He starts to move: **Kennedy** *gestures him back.*

Moore (*approaching*)   You mustn't touch that, sir. The man is dead.

Broome   If it's as you say, you've nought to fear: the man's unburied, the rites unsaid ...

He prises back the lid: the relatives call out, thrust back by **Kennedy** *with his sword.* **Mathew** *gestures round the cart.*

Broome   What's this?

Moore *doesn't answer.*

Broome   Your brother was a trooper, then?

Margaret   What?

Broome   Age thirty-four or five ...

Margaret   What?

Broome   And died from what?

Margaret   Old age ...

Broome   I'd say from a knife around his neck.

Margaret   What's this?

Broome Lean over, woman ... You must have a look.

Margaret Oh, *God*.

Joan No.

Broome (*to* **Moore**) I see no surprise in you, old man.

Logan Jesus, now, O'Halloran: but look at this.

O'Halloran A man as big as a mountain we've been towing round all day.

Kennedy So this is what they've done.

Broome If you'd said a trooper, we might have let you pass ... But to hide a corpse away: it brings one thought to mind.

Margaret (*to* **Moore**) Tell him. Tell him. We've never seen this thing before ... Never. Not anywhere ... I swear to God ... These men! What have you done with them?

O'Halloran To Jesus, now: we've never even looked.

Logan You've slept beside the cart yourself.

O'Halloran The stench an' all ...

Logan 'A sacred smell': I've heard you use the words yourself.

Proctor The nails have not been touched till now ...

Morgan This splintered wood is fresh.

O'Halloran But no one's touched the box at all.

Logan You see: we were on our way to market, sir ...

O'Halloran That's right.

Logan My friend and I: and this gentleman here was passing by ...

O'Halloran Asked us if we'd give a lift.

Logan The lady's tears – my God, your honour: you've never seen the like.

O'Halloran Pouring down her cheeks, they were.

Logan And one or two other places, now, besides.

O'Halloran I've never seen so many tears.

Logan No. No.

O'Halloran Not since your mother died.

Logan That's right.

Broome And so this corpse was invisibly transported, miraculously placed inside the wood and your aged, lightweight brother – if such a man existed which I doubt – with the same astonishing dexterity . . . passed out.

Moore I've nothing to say.

Margaret (*to* **Broome**) My father died. I watched them place him in the box myself . . . Joan . . . Even Mathew . . . he'd tell you if he could.

Mathew *nods, evidently agreeing, gesturing at the box.*

Margaret What're you all silent for? . . . Joan? . . . Uncle?

Pause.

Have you seen this man before?

Mathew, *dancing round the cart, is nodding, pointing at the box.*

Margaret What is he? . . . Where's my father gone?

Broome Madam: these questions are no concern of mine. The evidence is plain to see: a murdered corpse, moving furtively between the lines: you'll come with us. We'll leave the body here . . . These men can dig a grave.

O'Halloran What's that? What's that?

Logan Not us?

O'Halloran To Jesus, now, your honour . . .

Logan We've never seen the man before.

Morgan   If we dig a grave, then, can we go?

Broome   You'll break down branches ... Dig with that
... When the corpse is covered you'll come with us ...

O'Halloran   To God, then, Logan: what a mess.

Morgan   Didn't I tell you we should never have stayed
before.

Logan   Chamberlain, you know: you haven't said a word.

Chamberlain   There's no word to say: we do as the
soldier says.

The men depart.

Margaret *has stepped back from the cart: she leans on* **Joan**.

Moore *stands immobilised by the cart:* **Mathew** *still dances round
it, gesturing.*

As the men move off **Proctor** *moves over to the women.*

Proctor   There's nothing you can do now, you know ...

They make no response.

It's no good grieving: the dead are dead.

O'Halloran   And so are we, my friend: this time
tomorrer, I'm thinking ... We'll be looking for a box
ourselves.

They move off.

Light fades.

Scene Seven

The light comes up.

Chamberlain, O'Halloran, Logan, Proctor *and*
Morgan *are crouched together, linked by a rope.*

O'Halloran   They don't take any prisoners here.

Morgan   What's that?

O'Halloran   Ask Chamberlain: he knows.

Chamberlain *makes no answer.*

O'Halloran   They travel light.

Logan   No excess baggage.

O'Halloran   Take us out into the woods . . . (*Makes a splitting sound.*)

Logan   That's right.

Chamberlain   I think we ought to agree on a single alibi while we have the chance.

Logan   What alibi?

O'Halloran   What chance?

Chamberlain   That we were travelling away from the war.

Morgan   Like refugees.

O'Halloran   Five men, you mean. . . ?

Logan   Five stalwart men.

O'Halloran   Five stalwart men, you mean, like us. . . ?

Logan   We could say we were going to enlist, you know . . . On the Big One's side, that is, not ours.

O'Halloran   And we'll be bottled up in armour, then, as soon as not . . .

Logan   Pushed out.

O'Halloran   Blown up.

Logan   Ones like us they put out first . . .

O'Halloran   To see which way the shrapnel bursts . . .

Logan   Fodder for the guns: he's right.

O'Halloran   Nevertheless, there, Logan . . . It's our only chance.

Proctor Can you shift your allegiance, then, as easily as that?

Logan When there's a sword dangling by my throat I can shift it any way you like . . . Come on . . . come on: you can test it if you want.

Chamberlain I think it's better that we act alike: we were moving from the war. It's up to them to prove us wrong.

Morgan Proof? What proof? They'll need no proof. A corpse like the one we had. One look at that: you could see his face. The verdict's spoken, man, before we step outside.

Logan I can see that trooper's features right enough . . . puffed up . . . I thought he had a mouth, festering, beneath the opening where his real one stood: grinning, he was, from ear to ear, his head tossed back . . .

Proctor We've heard enough.

Logan How they got him in I've no idea.

O'Halloran Methinks I've seen the man before.

Morgan Before?

O'Halloran Up here. (*He nods his head.*) The description of a tale I heard.

Proctor Listen . . .

Chamberlain There's someone coming back . . .

They wait.

Kennedy *hurls in* **Moore**.

Kennedy Get in, old fool: and wait with these . . .

Morgan And are we likely to be getting out, then, soon?

O'Halloran Out and into something worse.

Kennedy *fastens the old man to the rope.*

Proctor Where are the women, then?

Kennedy Out there.

Proctor Waiting to be questioned, too?

A cry off.

O'Halloran Not waiting long . . .

Logan And who's in next?

Kennedy The next I call . . . And until I do . . . From none of you mun I hear a word.

Morgan What's happened to the madman, then?

Kennedy *looks back, doesn't answer: goes.*

Kennedy The afflicted one: he got away . . .

Logan Away?

Proctor He won't get far: they'll bring him back.

Morgan Did you tell them all you knew, then, man?

Moore I did. (*They look to him.*) Of you: I hardly said a word: we met by the road, that's all. By chance.

Morgan The corpse: the corpse: didn't they ask you what you knew of that?

Moore I told them.

Morgan Go on. Go on.

Moore I put it in the box myself . . .

Proctor Your niece – the woman – she never knew?

Moore *shakes his head.*

O'Halloran Nor Joan.

Moore Nor Joan . . . we panicked when the troopers came. My brother was already dead, the lid in place . . . My niece's daughter came – There was a trooper, already

dead, lying in the hedge beyond the yard . . . Killed: I
could see that at a glance. If they found him there . . . I
took him up: while the women were distracted, hiding food,
what few possessions my brother had, I put him in the box
– I could think of nothing else – and put my brother back
into his bed . . . They searched the house: I took them to
the rooms upstairs: my niece, from grief, remained below
. . . I explained the box, my brother's corpse . . . They
never thought to look inside . . . All they wanted, you see,
was loot . . . and food . . . They came back in force, took
all we had . . .

Another cry off.

You see . . . (*He struggles.*) They believe she knows as
well . . .

Logan   There's nothing you can do, old man.

Pause.

Proctor   Didn't you ever tell her . . . All these days:
hauling the cart? Didn't you tell her it was another man
inside?

Moore   I hadn't the heart . . . Her mind was fastened on
the priest . . . Once that was done I knew she'd rest . . .
My brother I buried the night we left . . . He lies there,
now. She wouldn't have known . . . I think her mind has
turned. She's learned it all . . . Belief, you see, was the only
thing she had . . .

O'Halloran   Who killed the trooper? Did you find that
out?

Moore (*shakes his head*)   I thought it was the girl, at first
. . . But now. I know as little, or as much, as her . . .

Another cry off.

If I could ease my hands of this I'd go outside . . . I should
have said I'd killed the man myself . . . I never thought of
it until they led me out . . . I tried to shout . . . I've no
reason now to live . . . (*Struggles.*) I could exonerate them all

... What's this!

Another cry off.

Morgan (*pulled by the rope*)   Leave off, old man. There's nothing you can do.

Pause.

Chamberlain   The best we can do, I think, is go our separate ways ... Each tell the tale he wants.

Proctor   And you?

Chamberlain   I've got no choice ... I'll tell them who I am.

Proctor   I can't sit here ... sit still ... If the lunatic gets out, then so can I.

O'Halloran   Aye ... A fool gets out ...

Logan   And he's a fool ...

O'Halloran   And we're damn fools, I'm thinking, waiting to be shot.

Logan   Here! (*Warns.*) There's someone coming now ...

Chamberlain   Keep still.

A pause. **Margaret** *and* **Joan** *come in, separately, silent: heads bowed, dishevelled.*

Kennedy *follows them in.*

Joan *sinks down;* **Margaret** *still stands, abstracted.*

Kennedy   You ... You've most to say: we'll see you first.

O'Halloran   Me? Me? But I've nothing left to add.

Morgan   Take me, officer ... I'll go in first.

Kennedy *looks from one to the other: sees* **Morgan**'s *look.*

Kennedy   All right ... One by one – they'll scarcely mind.

Kennedy *releases* **Morgan**: *they go.*

Logan I don't trust that Morgan ... the greasy bastard.

O'Halloran I've half a mind he means to tell them first ... Put in a word, and beg them for release.

Moore Margaret ... Are you all right? I can scarcely see you, girl.

Margaret *makes no gesture.* **Joan**, *after a while, looks up.*

Joan I think ... my mother's mind has gone ... She started singing when they beat her worst.

Moore I should have thought. I should ... I could have said I killed the man.

Joan I said that too ... The one who caught us laughed. 'A girl like you?' he said. (*She looks across.*) They'd laugh at you ... 'A man', they'd say, 'as old as that?'

Moore I could have crept up ... I might have cut his throat behind.

Joan I said that, too ... Crept up on what? Across a hedge ... I told them how he lay ... 'Didn't any branches shake, or twigs or leaves, or was the man asleep, you think?' ... I said, 'Asleep.' ... 'Yet his pipe, a moment before, you said, was lit ...' Even then, I might have lied ... (*She shakes her head.*) I can't go on. I've nothing left ... He offered me – the officer – to take me to his tent out there ...

O'Halloran The next time he asks you'll have no choice.

Joan For that, he'd exonerate us both from blame. (*Indicates* **Margaret**.)

Moore Then, God: while you've still got a chance, my child ... what's that in preference to your mother's life?

Joan And you ... you'd be the prisoner then they'd have ... while I lie there and listen to the shot ...

Moore There's no shooting at this old man that's not already done ...

Joan   You did your best . . . you thought it right . . . But for the priest, it might have worked . . . As for compounding one tragedy with two . . . I'd rather join you in your grief than step aside . . .

She comes over to **Moore**, *kneeling, embracing him.*

Logan   They're back.

O'Halloran   What?

Logan   There's someone out there, beyond the lines.

Proctor   Not one of them.

O'Halloran   Not Morgan coming back?

Proctor   The fool.

Logan   What?

Proctor   The idiot.

O'Halloran   He's seen!

Proctor   No . . . He's creeping by the track . . .

Logan   What's that he's got?

O'Halloran   Between his teeth . . .

Logan   A knife, bejasus . . .

Proctor   You can see it in the light . . .

O'Halloran   Aye, there lies the cause, I think, of our bloody, botched-up tale.

They wait.

Mathew *comes in, sinks down, looks back: then comes across. He gestures with the knife: smiles, gestures, moving round.*

O'Halloran   There lies your cut-throat . . . if he only had a tongue to tell.

Logan   They'll find another trooper stretched out there, laughing through his throat, I think . . .

O'Halloran   He did it for the best, I haven't a doubt.

Logan   Aye!

He and **O'Halloran** *laugh between themselves.*

Proctor   Here ... Mathew ... *Mathew* ... Cut me free!

Gestures with the rope.

Mathew *dances round.*

Proctor   Cut me free...!

Logan   Don't ask the man: he'll stick it in your head.

Proctor   Here ... Mathew ...

O'Halloran   Ask the girl.

Proctor   Tell him ... ask him ... cut me free.

Joan   Mathew ... Let me have the knife.

Logan   He'll have your fingers off, at least ... Don't try and take the thing. Look out!

O'Halloran   He's got the glitter in his eye: God help the soldier boys he meets.

Proctor   There ... there ... just cut me free ...

Joan   Cut it, Mat ... Just cut the rope for me ...

He cuts the rope.

Proctor *gets up.*

Mathew *dances back: he stops.*

They wait.

Proctor   The knife ... and would you let me have the knife, then, Mat?

O'Halloran   He'll let you have it right enough ... Look out, then, man. Look out.

Proctor   Let's have a look, then, Mat ... Come on.

O'Halloran   Don't take the knife, for God's sake, man ...

Logan   If you're going, man, for God's sake go . . .

Proctor   I'm going armed: I can't go as I am . . . In the dark, with a knife, I stand a chance.

He dances at **Mathew**: *takes his arm. Much stronger, he wrenches free the knife.*

Logan   Bejasus, Mr Chamberlain . . . But there's a soldier for your fight . . . If you'd known he was at your side would you have waited back for us?

Proctor   Chamberlain: shall I cut you free?

Chamberlain   You're better on your own: one stands a chance, but two, no chance at all.

Proctor   Just say the word.

Chamberlain   I can hardly move . . . I've brought them here: I'll stay with these.

Proctor   O'Halloran?

O'Halloran   To God: but I stand more chance in here . . . I've never been one to go scrumping through a wood.

Proctor   Logan?

Logan   I'm not a military man, myself . . . (*To* **O'Halloran**.) No. No. One glance, I think, would tell you that.

O'Halloran   One glance, I think, without a doubt.

Proctor   Old man?

Moore *shakes his head.*

Joan (*as she meets* **Proctor**'*s glance, also shakes her head*)   You're better on your own . . . My mother I couldn't leave, at least.

Proctor (*indicating* **Mathew**)   I'll leave him here.

He fastens **Mathew** *to his place on the rope.*

When they count the heads don't say a word.

Chamberlain   Where do you hope to make for, then?

Proctor   I'll find the enlistment place. That's what I came to do . . .

Logan   When you get to the place, you know . . .

Proctor   What's that?

Logan   And they have a list, you see . . . *Logan.*

O'Halloran   Tell them what occurred.

Proctor   I see.

O'Halloran   Tell them to put a line right through . . . O'Halloran, I think, you'll find there, too.

Proctor   I will . . . (*Looks round, determined.*) I'll go the way the fool came in.

Chamberlain   Good luck.

Proctor   Aye. I'll need it. (*Goes.*)

They watch, but for **Margaret** *and* **Moore***, and* **Mathew***, who struggles with the rope.*

Logan   He's through.

O'Halloran   He's not.

Logan   He is.

O'Halloran   You're right.

Logan   My God.

O'Halloran   The bloody fool.

Logan   He is.

O'Halloran   Shan't ever see his like.

Logan   No, no.

O'Halloran   A soldier, Chamberlain, through and through.

Chamberlain   I believe you're right.

Logan   Saw it when we met.

O'Halloran   One thought inside his head.

Logan   Just one.

O'Halloran   Leaves all the rest . . .

Logan   Uncluttered.

O'Halloran   A man of action.

Logan   Every time.

Chamberlain (*still looking off*)   He's gone into the darkness now . . .

Pause.

They wait, gazing off.

Silence.

Moore   Margaret? Won't you sit down, girl?

Joan *has moved to* **Margaret**: *she takes her hand.*

Joan   Let's sit beside the rest . . . There's nothing left to do.

Margaret   They lie there now . . . unblessed . . . Two fathers dead . . . two husbands, sons and brothers . . .

O'Halloran   What church is it, that has to bless the dead?

Logan   Haven't they enough on their hands already without waitin' for a priest?

Margaret   He'll not enter into paradise without a priest.

Logan   We better be finding one ourselves, I think . . . I can hear the feller coming back. Look out.

O'Halloran   Keep that wriggling idiot in line: he'll have our one clear military genius caught before he's run a mile.

Kennedy (*entering*)   Stand up . . . Stand up . . . Up on your feet . . . All of you . . . You as well.

He's followed in by **Morgan**, *then* **Broome**.

They get up slowly: **Mathew**, *cowed, is last to rise.*

Broome   So you're the recruiting man they sent.

Chamberlain (*looks to* **Morgan**. *Then:*)   I am.

Broome   And these the particular specimens you chose.

Chamberlain   They're chosen by their faith and nothing more.

Broome   A soldier is a soldier – fate, not faith, casts him in the role he has ... Would a man like you not join our side?

Chamberlain   I would not.

Broome   Not even unto death.

Chamberlain (*pauses*)   Not even unto that.

Broome *watches him: moves on.*

Broome   And you?

O'Halloran   Oh ... oh ... If you're looking for recruits, your honour ...

Logan   I've always got the colours muddled up ...

O'Halloran   It's the uniforms, you see ...

Logan   Which side is which ...

O'Halloran   Left or right ...

Logan   Facing front or facing back.

O'Halloran   I could never decide, you see, myself ...

Logan   Always needed someone like your honour, your gracious worshipful honour, to do it for me.

O'Halloran   I'm sure, now, but this was the very spot we meant.

Logan   The one we aimed for all the time.

O'Halloran Set on the track the day we left . . . pointed in the wrong direction.

Logan *This* is the place! I think you're right.

Broome And this?

Kennedy This isn't the man we left . . . The rope's been cut!

O'Halloran He dealt us a terrible blow . . .

Logan He did.

O'Halloran He had a knife – would you believe it – all the time.

Logan When no one's looking . . .

O'Halloran Cuts the rope.

Logan Captured this raving lunatic here . . .

O'Halloran Set him in his place.

Logan And went.

Kennedy Guard! (*Goes off.*)

O'Halloran Would we go with him?

Logan Would we not.

O'Halloran This is the army we intended all the time.

Logan If the man had only thought.

O'Halloran It might have been the one he wants himself.

Broome Is this the fool who ran off from the cart?

O'Halloran It is . . . And the one who did the crime at that.

Logan Putting two and two together . . .

O'Halloran Not that we'd know the facts, you see . . .

Logan Your honour . . .

O'Halloran Your worshipful grace . . .

Logan More a matter of speculation . . .

O'Halloran Speculation . . .

Logan Speculation there, I think you're right.

Kennedy (*returning*) They'll have him back . . . He can't have travelled far.

Broome These two can serve us . . . Cut them free. (*To* **Chamberlain**.) And you, and the old man there, we'll bind afresh.

Joan No . . . There's no need to bind a man as old as this.

Broome I think we have the culprit here . . . I believe your mother's story, girl. Grief like that, I'm sure, is not pretence.

Moore It's true . . . I killed him by the hedge.

Joan No.

Moore The girl: she found him . . . nothing else.

Joan He could never kill a man! He can't!

Kennedy *starts to take him out.*

Moore Joan . . . it's better that I go like this . . . Just think of me: I'm going gladly . . . (*Goes to her.*) What other role could this poor body have. I've done with life.

Broome Take him out!

Kennedy *thrusts* **Moore** *out.*

Broome As for you . . . and your mother . . . I shall set you free . . . The idiot too . . . He can do no worse than jabber his silence in some other camp . . . (*To* **Chamberlain**.) And as for you: your head we'll carry through the villages on a pike and announce the end of one recruiting-drive with the beginning of another . . . The old man's too we'll set up on a pike and travelling a little in advance allow it to proclaim the end of all men who might be tempted to take a trooper's life ... But as for now ... Three troops for one ...

Logan   That's right. Three. Three. That's quite correct.

Broome   If Mr Morgan here will lead the way.

O'Halloran   Ah, a man with a level head at last.

Exit.

Fade.

Act Two

Scene One

O'Halloran *and* **Logan** *enter, attired as soldiers.*

O'Halloran   You see, you see, now: lost again.

Logan   I'm sure this is the path we should have taken.

O'Halloran   If only armies would stand like men ... put out two fists, you know, and fight ... all these furtive shifts about ...

Logan   Two hours ago I could have told you where I was.

O'Halloran   Outflank them to the left, he said.

Logan   Ah, now ... Are you sure it wasn't the right?

O'Halloran   Right or left ... at no time in the centre where it counts.

Logan   In the centre, of course, he stands himself.

O'Halloran   While all goes on to left and right ...

Logan   And where the armies should have met ...

O'Halloran   Stands no one but himself ...

Logan   And the other chief, of course.

O'Halloran   That's right.

Logan   The best thing we can do ... (*Sits down.*)

O'Halloran   You're right ... (*Lies down.*)

Sounds of cannon off.

Logan   Ah, to God: they chose a day.

O'Halloran   They did.

Logan   Not a breath o' wind ...

O'Halloran   Not a drop o' cloud.

They stretch out.

Logan   If I could get this off I think I'd bathe.

O'Halloran   If I thought I could get it on again.

Logan   The logic, you see, of being trussed up.

Cannon off.

Was that a bird?

O'Halloran   I think it was.

Logan   The noise beyond . . .

O'Halloran   Obliterates the sound.

Logan   At least one thing . . .

O'Halloran   Three meals a day.

Logan   Three meals a day and a drop to drink.

O'Halloran   A roof above your head at times.

Cannon off.

Jasus: if they'd turn that off. (*Yawns, stretches, lying back.*)

Logan   A day like this, I wouldn't mind . . .

O'Halloran   No, no . . .

Logan   Making the effort . . .

O'Halloran   That's right . . .

Logan   To stay alive. (*Yawns hugely: settles back.*)

They doze.

Pause.

Morgan *enters, similarly attired, a superior rank.*

Morgan   And what the hell's going on down here?

Logan   To God . . . It's the commander-in-chief himself.

O'Halloran   To Jesus, Morgan ... but you made me start.

Morgan   You're supposed to outflank the place, not stretch out on the ground.

O'Halloran   Now would that be to the left, or right?

Morgan   The right ...

Logan   That's where, you see, we went astray.

O'Halloran   I told him to the left.

Logan   No, no ... *I* to the left ... I believe you said the right.

O'Halloran   No, no ... I to the left, I believe and Logan to the right.

Logan   Nevertheless, I'll take the blame.

O'Halloran   No, no, but I'll take it on myself. I shall.

Morgan   Whatever the way, you'll follow me. Pick up your weapons ... Get up off the ground.

Logan   Oh, dear ...

O'Halloran   Oh, my.

Logan   No sooner settled down.

They start to rise.

O'Halloran   A pitiless man.

Logan   He is at that.

O'Halloran   Where's the Morgan we used to know ...

Logan   Beneath those superannuated stripes.

Proctor *comes in, attired as one of the opposing forces.*

Proctor   Stand fast ...

O'Halloran   To God ... An enemy at last.

Logan   And fierce, to boot.

O'Halloran   And fierce, at that.

Morgan   Put down your arms: you're outnumbered three to one.

Proctor   Outnumbered, but not outfought: do you think I give a damn!

Logan   Proctor, to God! 'Tis the blacksmith man himself.

O'Halloran   See . . . your friends: you've found your friends at last.

Proctor   No friends of mine in rags like that.

Logan   Oh, God: another monomanic fool . . .

O'Halloran   See . . . see . . . beneath this mask . . .

Logan   O'Halloran . . .

O'Halloran   Logan.

Proctor   I recognise you well enough.

O'Halloran   And Morgan.

Proctor   And Morgan . . .

Logan   Promoted . . . Oh, promoted above the heads of O'Halloran and me.

Proctor   Lay down your arms, or strike at that.

O'Halloran   To God, but we'd hardly touch a friend . . .

Logan   Or foe.

O'Halloran *and* **Logan** *toss down their arms.*

Proctor   Allegiance, I see . . . like the coat upon your back . . . tossed on or off, according to the cloud or light.

O'Halloran   Oh, we have a great interest . . .

Logan   In seeing the rights and wrongs . . .

O'Halloran   Of every side.

Logan   There are two sides at least to every question.

O'Halloran   Three or four, if the truth were known.

Logan   Only a fool would come down on one.

O'Halloran   While a real man at least comes down on two.

Proctor   Morgan has gone too far to change his suit . . . it's veritably fastened round his neck with braid . . . each stripe a stroke of treason to our cause . . . Well, Morgan: let's see your sword unravel that. (*Puts up his sword.*)

They fight. Cannons rumble off.

Logan   Ah, now . . . oh, now . . .

O'Halloran   Oh, dear . . . oh, dear . . .

Logan   Don't take it seriously now . . .

O'Halloran   'Tis only war.

Logan *and* **O'Halloran** *dance out of the way: they alternatively cover their eyes and watch.*

Logan   Oh, dear . . . oh, dear . . .

O'Halloran   But what a sight.

Logan   Friends: remember . . . men beneath the shirt.

Proctor   No man is this . . . A rat, and turncoat. Nothing else.

Morgan   And this an ass: allegiance fastened like a shroud around his head.

Proctor   'Tis a flag of honour you see, my friend.

Morgan   'Tis a blindfold, masking common sense.

O'Halloran   All this, all this: and poetry too!

Morgan *and* **Proctor** *fight on.*

Logan   'Tis a mystifying thing is war.

O'Halloran   Once killed, you know, there's nothing else.

Proctor   I'd rather die like this than linger in a bed . . .

or switch my side for advancement o'er my friends.

They fight with shouts and groans.

Logan Idealists and opportunists.

O'Halloran We must hold aloof.

Morgan *falls:* **Proctor** *stands over him with a sword.*

Proctor Do you yield, then, Morgan ... traitor ... rat
... Or shall I pass this through you to the ground?

Morgan I yield. I yield.

Logan A sensible man, at last.

As **Morgan** *rises he tries to strike* **Proctor** *down.*

O'Halloran To God and Jesus, man: look out!

Proctor *turns: runs* **Morgan** *through.*

Proctor Traitors never learn until their crime is past.
(*Sheathes his sword.*)

Logan Your honour, then ...

O'Halloran We better find our path. (*Retreating.*)

Logan Through the forest wend our way ...

O'Halloran Weaponless ...

Logan Bereft of arms.

Proctor You'll come with me.

O'Halloran But shouldn't we trot off home ... You,
me, Logan: the three of us are nothing but village-men at
heart ... This war ...

Cannon roar.

We had a part ...

Logan The role's expired.

O'Halloran There's nothing left ...

Logan We could excuse ourselves ...

O'Halloran   Retire . . .

Logan   No one the wiser . . .

O'Halloran   Nor better off.

Logan   Nor worse.

Proctor   If everyone thought like you there'd be no war
. . . No principle, honour, virtue . . . no cause to raise a
man at all.

Logan   Ah, but many to celebrate its absence with.

O'Halloran   Unmaimed.

Logan   Unkilled.

O'Halloran   Unblinded.

Logan   Take Morgan here . . .

O'Halloran   Three stripes.

Logan   A little longer he might have counted more . . .
while here, you see . . . (*Indicating his own arm.*) No mark at
all.

Proctor   I see no principle of any sort in that.

Logan   Principle, you see, is like a cart: jump on, jump
off . . . Poor Morgan fell between . . . while we: the slightest
commotion knocks us off . . . no principle, you see, can
hold us long . . . no principle, for instance, Proctor, leaves
its mark . . .

Proctor   The principle of self-preservation, I imagine:
nothing else.

Logan   What's preserved of Morgan, now, but these? . . .
the stripes, the boots, the sword . . . a rag to hand on now
to someone else . . . some deluded, animated corpse –
waves them in the air and screams, dying or dismembered
or blinded, for a cause . . . And when one cause expires
but its opposite begins . . . Proctor's flag today . . .
tomorrow . . . this.

Proctor   You'll come with me . . . without ideals no man can live.

Logan   And with ideals we end like this. (*Gestures round.*)

They go.

Light fades.

Scene Two

Light comes up.

Proctor *comes on, tired, his uniform loosened: still authoritative, stern.*

He's followed by **O'Halloran** *and* **Logan**: *they've discarded their uniform to varying degrees.*

O'Halloran   The battle's like a carrot to the man . . . the faster he goes, the quicker it passes on.

Proctor   It's a rout . . . one side has fled – the other's given chase.

Logan   On horse, or machines, I'd say: but not on foot . . . (*Sits.*) Dispose of us both, then, Proctor . . . I'll not move another step from here.

O'Halloran (*sinks down*)   To God, a military boot is that: a hole big enough to let another foot stick out.

Proctor   There's a farmhouse over there. We'll make for that.

O'Halloran   You'll have to carry him . . . and me.

Proctor   I'll reconnoitre it . . . Do you give your word you'll stay?

Logan   I'll stay.

O'Halloran   I'll stay . . . I'll stay beside my feet at least . . . and where my feet are now . . . I'll rest.

Logan   Go on then, feller, for we'll never leave.

Proctor *goes.*

O'Halloran   'Tis a dishevelled bloody place at that.

Logan   No roof.

O'Halloran   Two walls . . .

Logan   The other two removed.

O'Halloran   A damn great bomb, I think, has tumbled down the thatch.

Logan   To God . . . (*He stretches out.*)

O'Halloran   Hauled between armies . . .

Logan   Like fish inside a net.

O'Halloran   'Tis a disagreeable business, war . . . when one side wins, the other breaks its neck . . . To God . . . but don't look now . . . That ijit's back . . . the one we knew before.

Mathew *has come on, dishevelled, carrying a long, thin load.*

Logan   Has he got a knife?

O'Halloran   A sword.

Logan   Holy Mother . . . Captured by a madman now!

O'Halloran   I think he's smiled . . .

Logan   Or grinned . . .

O'Halloran   I can't be sure . . . Your honour . . . don't you remember us, your grace . . . To Jasus, Logan: but he's coming up.

Logan   And where's the Captain now? . . . About to lose two prisoners and he's vanished out of sight . . . (*Calls.*) Proctor!

O'Halloran   Proctor!

Logan   No, no . . . it is a smile, you're right.

O'Halloran   What I thought was a sword is a loaf of bread.

Logan   Food . . . but, Jesus: what a sight.

They've got up hastily.

Mathew, *nodding and grinning, offers the loaf.*

Logan   O'Halloran. I must be dreaming yet . . .

O'Halloran   Tell me if I'm wrong . . .

Logan   Isn't that the girl herself?

Joan *enters, followed by* **Proctor**. *She carries a pitcher of water.*

Joan   I've brought you this: water, I'm afraid: we've nothing else.

They take the pitcher as greedily as they've taken the bread.

O'Halloran   To God: but that's the loveliest stuff on earth. (*Drinks.*)

Joan   I sent Mat out: the soldiers came . . . the bread was all we had to hide.

Proctor   The soldiers . . . were their coats . . . like theirs . . . or mine?

Joan   Like yours . . . or theirs . . . They look alike.

Proctor   Woman. This coat is different from the rest!

Logan   Do you want a drink? Or do we throw the rest away?

Proctor *hesitates, then takes it.*

O'Halloran   Do you want the bread, or not?

Proctor *takes it.*

Joan   The battle's gone . . . the soldiers went away . . . the fields are burnt . . . the house is down.

Logan (*indicating* **Proctor**)   New principles, I can see, must be fashioned now.

O'Halloran   The war has gone . . .

Logan   And left its principal behind.

O'Halloran I can see the fellers now . . .

Logan 'And where's the man with all the stripes?'

O'Halloran 'Proctor was the name.'

Logan 'Fell on the field . . . or deserted, sir.'

O'Halloran Which is all the same when the fighting's done.

Logan When the fighting's o'er, and the battle won.

O'Halloran *and* **Logan** *laugh:* **Proctor** *stands as if immobilised.*

O'Halloran And you, young lady: is your mother well?

Logan Better off than she was before?

Joan She died – the night we left camp . . . I think her brain was seized . . . we brought her on the cart . . . she lies out there . . . beside her father now . . .

They pause.

Proctor *removes his cap: sits down.*

Logan And now the sword.

O'Halloran Without his principles, you mean . . . he might bend the path.

Logan Divert it, as it were, from its original course.

Proctor (*to* **Joan**) Will you stay here?

Joan We can come with you.

Proctor We'll find a place where no one fights . . . with words, with ideas, with philosophies . . . but not with these. (*Kicks his sword aside.*)

Logan One madness exits but to greet the next.

Proctor We'll go that way . . . yonder . . . where the wood's untouched . . . We'll find a place where we can rest a while . . . I'm tired. I've had enough of war . . . We'll find a place for moral argument.

They go: **Proctor** *leading, followed by* **Joan** *and* **Mathew**. **Logan** *and* **O'Halloran** *follow last.*

Light fades.

Scene Three

Light comes up: muted.

They enter.

Joan   I think the wood grows thicker here . . .

Logan   The path, I see, is fadin' too.

Proctor   From the top of the hill the way seemed clear.

O'Halloran (*coming in last*)   Clear from above, but muddled once below.

A wild figure leaps in: a huge shriek: it whirls a sword. Long-haired, almost naked, **Cleet** *flashes his sword before them.*

Cleet   Stand fast, you slimy bastards! . . . Did you think I'd let you through?

O'Halloran   Through?

Logan   Through what, your honour?

Cleet   Through woods I call my own.

O'Halloran   We were not aware . . .

Logan   We were distinctly unaware . . .

O'Halloran   That these beautiful trees . . .

Logan   Were all your own.

Cleet *flourishes his sword more wildly still: he leaps round them with fresh impetus.*

O'Halloran   We thought, that is . . .

Logan   They belonged to the Big One, then.

Cleet   The Big One, did you?

O'Halloran The one who . . . won the war.

Logan That's right.

Cleet *seems less disposed towards them now than ever.*

O'Halloran *and* **Logan** *glance at one another.*

O'Halloran The one, of course . . . to whom we're indisposed.

Cleet Indisposed to the Big One, are ye?

Logan The one who won the war?

Cleet That's right. (*He waits.*)

O'Halloran If he's the One . . .

Logan We think he is . . .

O'Halloran He's the One to whom . . .

Logan With whom . . .

O'Halloran For whom . . .

Cleet You're on the Big One's side, or mine?

Logan Oh, definitely . . .

O'Halloran Yours, your honour . . .

Logan Your grace . . .

O'Halloran Your worship . . .

Logan Every time.

Cleet And these?

O'Halloran Oh, these are friends of ours . . .

Logan Of his . . .

O'Halloran Of yours.

Logan Of mine.

Cleet I'll take you to our camp-place, then. My name is Cleet. One word of where we go, of how we get there, of what it looks like once we're fast inside . . .

O'Halloran Oh, now . . . not a word.

Logan Not a murmur.

O'Halloran Not a sound.

Logan Shan't say a thing.

O'Halloran To God, your honour . . .

Logan You can trust us . . .

O'Halloran Every time.

Cleet *turns to lead the way.*

O'Halloran To God and Jesus, now: what's this: a
madman clears the field apace; where thistles, grass and
nettle grew a second madman plants the weeds anew.

They go.

Light fades.

Scene Four

Light comes up.

They're sitting in a circle.

In addition to **Cleet** *there are two other wild and heavily-armed
figures:* **Wallace** *and* **Drake**.

Cleet These are my comrades you can see gathered here.

Logan Armed for a resurrection . . .

O'Halloran Insurrection . . .

Logan Insurrection . . . I can see that at a glance.

Wallace The woods on either side are filled with men.

Drake And beside each man . . .

Wallace A sword.

Drake   A gun.

O'Halloran   And these are against the Big One, too?

Wallace   The one who took the land.

O'Halloran   And when the Big One's beaten, then?

Drake   You'll see a place where everything is shared.

Wallace   No land, no property, not common to us all.

Logan   But when the insurrection starts . . .

O'Halloran   With the ones, you see, you've dispossessed . . .

Cleet   We'll stamp them out.

Drake   A flame like ours is always lit.

Wallace   Who's heard of the thing that can extinguish it?

O'Halloran   To Jesus: but manic fools unite . . .

Logan   The better to prolong the fight.

Cleet   Are you with us, then? (*Rises: sword drawn, stands over them.*) Or are you set against?

Proctor   I'm tired of war . . . We travelled to a place, I thought, where men took sides with words, not swords.

Wallace   There is no such place.

Drake   No words stake out their claim but swords are not drawn up behind.

Joan   Yet if we don't . . . Or if we can't.

Wallace   No don't, or can't.

Joan   Yet take up neither side . . .

Proctor   But stand aloof . . .

Joan   Looking to our own and nothing else.

Cleet   Your own is ours . . . and ours is yours to share.

Drake   Our side, or theirs. (*Draws out his sword too.*)

Proctor We fall between the two . . .

Vast explosions on either side.

Cleet To arms! The troops have reached the woods!

Other explosions.

To the trees! To the trees, God damn you! No prisoners, now! We fight them to the end!

The three figures rush off in separate directions: cannon, firing off.

O'Halloran To Jesus, now . . .

Logan Come on . . .

Joan Let's fly . . .

O'Halloran Proctor . . . are you going to join the men?

Joan With us . . . For God's sake, Proctor, fly!

They dash off, separately.

Mathew! . . . This way . . . Mathew! With us!

Fade.

Scene Five

Light comes up.

Proctor and **Joan** *rest on the ground.*
Mathew *is making a fire, cooking, some distance off.*

Joan Has he prepared the food?

Proctor It won't be long.

Joan Are we safe this far away?

Proctor We'll journey on.

Joan Or back.

Proctor Or back?

Joan To the farm . . . there's nowhere else . . . You could build a smithy: we could start again.

Proctor   Rebuild the place?

Joan   Re-sow the fields ... build up the hedges ... repair the thatch ... fashion walls.

Proctor   And have a child?

Joan   That too.

Pause.

Proctor   It's hard ... (*He moves aside.*) I'm used to having conviction on my side ... badges, stripes, emblems, that tell me who and what and where I am ... To live like this ... (*He shakes his head.*) Subversionists and spies.

Joan   Or lovers, who would have no thought ...

Proctor   But for themselves.

Joan   What lover, in loving, does not love others too.

Proctor   Aye ...

She holds him.

Mathew *crosses with food: hesitates; retreats.*

Light fades.

Scene Six

Light comes up.

A **Boatman** *who poles his boat across a river, now standing on the bank.*

Logan *and* **O'Halloran** *enter.*

Logan   To God, but running wears me down ... surrender, I think, 'd be an altogether less demanding thing.

O'Halloran   Bone, and a minimum of bone, and skin ...

Logan   And that's an optimum account.

O'Halloran   To God, and all that water too ...

Boatman   Are you the ones that passed through here before?

O'Halloran   Reduced in number now, you see.

Boatman   What happened to your companions? The girl?

Logan   The girl has gone.

O'Halloran   The blacksmith too.

Logan   Escorted by the madman.

Boatman   The rest?

O'Halloran   Are dead.

Boatman   The mother, too?

Logan   If we told the tale, it would never end.

Boatman (*shakes his head*)   Many the men who cross this stream ... and many the history they have to tell ... the world's abuse, the world's acclaim ... they set their paths by distant lights ... while I, day in, day out, navigate between two shadowy shores ...

O'Halloran   Oh, indispensable, despite the tedium of the task.

Boatman   And overlooked ... the use is all: without the boat they're lost.

Logan   A boat, I can see, we shall have to build ourselves.

O'Halloran   Or swim.

Boatman   Too deep: too fast.

Logan   And men like us?

Boatman   Without the price no man can pass.

Logan   To God, O'Halloran ... A job.

O'Halloran   And here I'd been thinking we might last without.

Logan   We'll travel back.

O'Halloran   A soldier's pay.

Logan   A labourer's hire.

O'Halloran   When we've got the price . . .

Logan   We'll cross the stream.

Boatman   When that day comes – you'll find me here.

They turn away.

Logan   I had a dream.

O'Halloran   Ah, yes.

Logan   I heard a choir . . .

O'Halloran   Singing.

Logan   Very loud and clear.

O'Halloran   And when the singing stopped . . .

Logan   A bird.

O'Halloran   And when you looked?

Logan   I saw it perched.

O'Halloran   The topmost branch . . .

Logan   Of a nearby tree . . .
You've heard this dream before, I think.

O'Halloran   I have.

Logan   No need to tell you how it ends.

They go.

Boatman *waits.*

Stage darkens.

Act Three

Scene One

Joan *enters.*

Proctor *with a scythe.*

Proctor How's the child?

Joan She's fine . . . See . . .

Proctor Running in the fields.

Joan The country's quiet.

Proctor The crops swell out the barn . . . The tenancy is paid.

Joan The smithy crackles with its stove all day.

Proctor The dead: familiar ghosts . . .

Joan Not demons, screaming in the mind.

Proctor The house filled out with children's cries.

Joan And here two labourers, worthy of their hire.

They laugh.

O'Halloran *and* **Logan** *come on.*

O'Halloran Good evening, your honour.

Logan Missis . . . It's a lovely night.

Proctor Are you going far – or home to bed?

Logan We're travelling, let me see . . .

O'Halloran To the nearest bar.

Joan And savings . . . that you came to make?

Logan Saved for the day . . .

O'Halloran But spent throughout the night.

Proctor We'll see you in the morning, then?

Logan Aye. God willing.

O'Halloran If the sun hangs right.

They go.

Joan Stars.

Proctor And moon.

Joan Shaped like a scythe.

Proctor A sickle: angled at the chimney, then ... (*Looks round after a while.*) I'll call the child.

Joan Time to retire ... I'll set the table.

Proctor Bolt the door.

Joan And settle in our haven, then.

They go.

Light fades.

Scene Two

Light comes up.

Cleet, *bloodied, bandaged, helped by* **Wallace**. **Drake** *has come ahead.*

Drake Here's a place.

Wallace We'll hide in here.

Drake Warm and dry.

Cleet A barn ... I can scarcely see.

They ease him down.

Wallace The troopers ...

Cleet Are they far behind?

Drake Not far.

Wallace   They'll never search in here.

Cleet   There's someone there! ... Listen ... (*Points blindly.*)

Mathew *rises from where he's been asleep.*

Cleet   Who is it?

Wallace   An idiot, going by his stare.

Drake   He's armed.

Wallace   A knife.

Cleet   Disarm him, then ...

Drake *and* **Wallace** *advance on* **Mathew**. *He turns and runs.*

Wallace   He's gone.

Cleet   Quick ... outside!

Drake   He'll not get far ... I'll take him in the night.

He goes.

Cleet *lies back.*

Cleet   That battle ... Wallace? I thought we'd see them run.

Wallace   We did.

Cleet   Aye ... And turn ... in greater number still.

Wallace   Set-pieces are not the way to fight ... out on the plain, in open fields ...

Cleet   We can't live in the woodland all our lives: I thought the time had come ... we'd see men rise, flock around us ... As it is ... they work and sleep ... think little ... feel nothing ... the profit of their work drawn off ... quiescent ... dreamers ... full of beer and bread ...

Wallace   What's that? (*Draws his sword, rising.*)

Proctor *has entered. He's followed in by* **Mathew**.

Proctor   This is my barn ... Without my permission you've no rights in here.

Wallace   Our barn ... This is our barn ...

Cleet   I must commend you on the way it's kept.

Wallace   Well-stocked ...

Cleet   And warm.

Wallace   The roof well thatched.

Proctor   By my labour ... and by my effort ... By that of no one else.

Cleet   We had other work to do.

Proctor   Aye. I see.

Cleet   Which inflicts a heavier price than the one you're at.

Proctor   Not a price I asked, or set.

Cleet   But all would set the price who hold things to themselves.

Proctor   The things I've worked for I've fashioned by myself ...

Cleet   And family?

Proctor   For my wife and child.

Drake *comes in.*

Drake   I followed him in here ... I see he's fetched his master out.

Wallace   This man, I think, we've met before.

Drake   The one who's sick of war: you're right.

Wallace   He sets his sword aside ... and ploughs ... sets up his little household here ...

Drake   And thinks the world outside has died.

Cleet   There are men outside who have no land to till
... no crops to grow ... no wife to feed ... no child, no
house, no barn ... no bread ... no wine ... no place to
call their own. You have no answer, I can see, to that.

Proctor   What do you want of me? ... I'd rather join
that throng than fight again.

Cleet   And would a brave man play that part?

Proctor (*approaches*)   A brave man makes his life. He saves
it if he can ... Do you think one bloodied head ... a
thousand heads ... a mile of corpses ... will change by
one degree the world out there?

Wallace   The man's insane.

Cleet (*to* **Proctor**)   The world stands still ...

Proctor   As the top parts grow ... so do the branches
underneath ... A tree bears up its leaves ... hoists up its
branches ... and grows by the reaching out of its
extremities to the sun and sky ... You – you would have
us like a hedge ... hacked down each year to a common
height.

Wallace   The man is mad.

Cleet   And of oppression?

Proctor   One awards each man according to his need ...
change by degree ... a dead man is no longer fit for good
or ill: a live man, however hard, can be fashioned by his
will.

Cleet   And of those oppressed so hard that nature stops
their growth?

Proctor   I see no oppression harder than the one you
bring in here ... is life perfected by the loss of blood?
What world was made that wasn't unmade for its good?

Drake   We have another philosopher, Cleet, I see.

Cleet   Who casts his eye so far it overlooks our heads.

Proctor My eyes are cast about my feet – my hands, the soil, my wife, my child . . . my true barter with people of like mind. My toil, my labour . . . I carry revolution in my head, and heart . . . not streaked along a sword, or buried with the dead.

Wallace 'Tis cry and cry alike . . . the cry for equality is the loudest cry of all . . . Not for your barn, your labour, or your farm . . . but for the goodness that lends them to us all.

Proctor Have the barn . . . What's broken down by you I can build again.

Cleet Aye . . . 'tis destruction you see in me . . . and not the promotion of a higher cause.

Proctor One thing I've found of causes . . .

Cleet Aye?

Proctor No cause is greater than its means.

Cleet Oppressors are met by oppressor's schemes.

Proctor Then oppression makes reflections of itself – and calls it revolution . . . change . . . the end to discontent . . . And change it is . . . the beggar usurps the horseman and takes the whip himself.

Cleet *turns aside.*

Cleet All I have need of now is rest . . .

Proctor Well, rest I'll not deny . . . nor food . . .
Mathew: go to the house . . . water . . . and ointment to set a wound.

Mathew *goes.*

Proctor *kneels to look at* **Cleet***'s wound.*

Proctor Aye . . . it's bad enough . . . The flesh has healed . . . but the wound's begun to rot.

Drake Do you think the man will die?

Proctor It'll take a deeper thrust than that . . . My wife can set the wound.

Wallace And after that?

Proctor Ten days . . . a week . . .

Cleet We'll rest up here.

Drake And for your services . . .

Proctor No services are those that meet a need.

Light fades.

Scene Three

Light comes up.

Broome *enters: military figure, followed by* **Kennedy**.

Broome Aye . . . This is the place . . . the track leads here.

Joan (*enters*) Is there any way I can help you, sir?

Kennedy Aye . . . we're looking for a troop of men.

Broome One wounded, if not two at least.

Joan What kind of men?

Kennedy Insurrectionists . . .

Broome Subversionists . . .

Kennedy (*coming forward*) Anarchists: revolutionaries – men of simple mind.

Joan How do they appear?

Broome They wear no uniform of any kind.

Joan How does one describe them, then?

Kennedy They have no appearance, ma'am, but simplicity itself . . .

Broome   Dirt ... and a general air of infestation.

Kennedy   Evasiveness of manner ...

Broome   And the inability to look one directly in the eye.

O'Halloran *and* **Logan** *enter.*

O'Halloran   Good day, your honour.

Logan   Good day, your worship.

Kennedy   Good day, yourself.

Broome   Not these at least.

Logan   To God: but those are beautiful clothes you wear.

Kennedy   The same's for you, if you want to join.

O'Halloran   Oh, but we're well contented to work down here.

Logan   With no disrespect to yourself, that is.

Broome   We're looking for a troop of men.

Joan   The only men we have are these ... The idiot yonder ... and my husband in the fields.

Kennedy   Your husband's being brought in, I see.

Broome   The men have encircled the place: there's no retreat.

O'Halloran   To God ...

Logan   Another war sprung up!

Kennedy   What evidence have you found there, men?

Two **Soldiers** *enter with* **Proctor.**

First Soldier   Straw ...

Second Soldier   Stained with blood.

First Soldier   And dressings, sir ...

Second Soldier   The sign of habitation in the barn.

Kennedy   A hide-out, then.

O'Halloran   To God, your honour.

Logan   This is news to us.

Broome (*to* **Joan**)   Haven't I seen your face before?

Joan   You have.

Kennedy (*to* **Proctor**)   And yours too I thought I knew.

Broome   And these . . .

Kennedy   There's a familiar ring about the place . . .
Sergeant: tighten the cordon. Break the hedge . . . Set fire
to the barn . . . the house.

Joan   No!

Proctor   No!

O'Halloran   To Jesus: but we've just built up the
place . . .

Broome   Sheltering insurrectionists is a Federal crime . . .
your house is forfeit; your land as well . . . Corporal, take
these men in charge . . .

Joan   I have a child . . . For God's sake: let me at the
house!

Kennedy   The house is fired.

Logan   The flame leaps up the thatch . . .

Proctor   But let me near . . . let me in the house!

The **Soldiers** *hold him and* **Joan** *back as they call out and
scream.*

Joan   Oh, Jesus . . . O my child . . . if you have any pity
left!

Broome   Set light to the fields: we'll have these felons out
. . . no food or shelter: retreat turned into rout.

The light fades.

Scene Four

The light comes up.

Joan, **Proctor**, *stooped, broken,* **O'Halloran** *and* **Logan**, *followed by* **Mathew**, *form a line of figures that moves across the stage.*

Soldiers *guard them on either side.*

O'Halloran   Where are we bound to, Captain?

First Soldier   Corporal.

Logan   But you have the face . . .

O'Halloran   And bearing . . .

Logan   Of a more distinguished man, your grace.

Second Soldier   We're taking you where you'll cause no trouble.

Logan (*to* **O'Halloran**)   As safe as where we were before.

O'Halloran   Houses, are there?

First Soldier   Aye.

Logan   And fields?

Second Soldier   Aye. A place to work for sure.

The **Soldiers** *laugh.*

O'Halloran   To God: we had enough of that before.

Logan   Are there many people there like us, your grace?

First Soldier   Aye, don't worry . . . (*Laughs.*)

Second Soldier   You'll find there many more.

The **Soldiers** *laugh.*

Wallace *leaps on.*

Wallace   Lay down your arms! Stand back!

He's heavily armed: whirls sword.

O'Halloran   To Jesus: but we're overcome!

Drake, *similarly attired, darts on: he stabs the* **Second Soldier** *as he draws his sword.*

He leaps to the **First Soldier** *and with* **Wallace**, *runs him through.*

Logan   But God and Holy Mary: they never gave the man a chance.

Drake   Do you come with us . . . or join him there?

Wallace   No time for half-decisions now.

O'Halloran   Aye . . .

Logan   We're with you . . .

O'Halloran   Always was.

Proctor   I'll choose the sword.

Joan   He doesn't know his mind . . . He'll go with you.

Joan *has gone to* **Proctor**.

Wallace   And him? (*Looking at* **Mathew**.)

Drake   If he can wield a sword.

Logan   He's wielded knives with skill before.

Wallace   Then, welcome . . . comrades . . .

Drake   We'll make for Cleet.

Wallace   Tell them of our plans.

O'Halloran   And the remuneration, we hear, is very grand.

Drake   A better world!

Logan   A better world.

O'Halloran   A better world.

Logan   It's come to that.

They move off.

Light fades.

Scene Five

Light comes up.

Cleet *sits alone.*

Wallace *comes in.*

Wallace   They're here.

Cleet *gestures to send them in.* **Broome** *enters, followed by* **Kennedy**.

Broome   We've come with terms.

Cleet   I need no terms.

Kennedy   We hold the towns; we hold all the major routes and forts.

Cleet   And little else . . . you have no food. You've burnt up all the fields . . .

Broome   Nevertheless we come with terms . . . The state offers you a coalition.

Cleet   I need no coalition . . . coalesce with what? The people are disaffected . . . Look through these woods . . . an army made up from all your towns and forts . . . The battle's lost. Take off your medals. Join with us. Generals and captains are not political men. We hold no grudge. Exchange your uniform for one of ours and we'll march together to the city wall and proclaim our confederacy with such a shout that tyranny itself will come running out. What say you, men?

Broome (*looks to* **Kennedy**. *Then:*) Aye . . .

Cleet   And you?

Kennedy   Aye . . . Where the people lead . . . Then order follows.

Light fades.

Scene Six

Light comes up.

Proctor *sits on a stone, alone.*

Joan *comes in.*

Joan   The fool is ill.

Proctor *doesn't stir.*

Joan   I can't make out the cause.

Proctor   His mind has used him well . . . Depriving him of speech and thought.

Joan *leads* **Mathew** *on in a drooping condition.*

Joan   I think he sickens for what he had before.

Proctor   He sickens for his illness, then.

Joan   I'll take him back . . . We'll join the others . . . Build up, if not the old place, something new.

Proctor   Bend with the wind . . . While I sit like a rock . . . take on each storm as if it were the last . . .

Joan   But come with us . . .

Proctor   Like donkeys to a mill . . . Round . . . and round . . . and round, and round.

Joan   See: the idiot has brought us back his smile.

Proctor   Aye . . . he recognises his fellow madmen well.

Joan   The fruits of the labour, not the labouring, you thought were our reward.

Proctor   Does a man not set his eyes on the things he's laboured for?

Joan   No more than on a child that he sends out from his door: not his, but her life is the thing he's struggled for.

Proctor   It denies the principal thing in men . . .

Joan   It denies their arrogance and pride.

Proctor   Aye . . . but see new masters take up the things they won . . . new towns, new farms, new forts . . . new troops – old troopers with fresh harness on.

Joan   Let leaders lead: direct us as they will – support the good, and fight against the ill . . . what can't be taken is our joy in work . . . our life, like theirs, is forfeit in the end.

Proctor *shakes his head.*

Joan   But what you looked for was a kind of death – the uniform at first, and then a home – inviolable extremes that like a hearse can take you safely to a given end.

Proctor   I'll have no more of living as it comes . . . I must have goals, and ways and means . . . if men are victims what value are the things they struggle to?

Joan   I'll leave you here.

Proctor   The fool has turned his back.

Joan   He fights . . . and works . . . he sees his path . . .

Proctor   But inches from his head . . . I look for further goals than that.

Joan   The goal is in his heart . . . and mine.

Proctor   Aye . . . Well mine is turned to some vaster place than that.

She turns.

Mathew *has already turned: she follows him.*

Light fades.

Scene Seven

Light comes up.

Proctor *is kneeling.*

O'Halloran *and* **Logan** *enter.*

O'Halloran A preacher . . .

Logan Or a hermit.

O'Halloran The place is wild at that.

Logan The search for work has taken us further than we thought.

O'Halloran Away, or nearer . . .

Logan The searching's all that counts.

O'Halloran Your honour, then . . .

Proctor *stirs.*

Logan What prays your honour to, so well?

Proctor I pray to God.

O'Halloran The one above . . .

Logan Or the one we see around?

Proctor I pray to be illuminated, friend.

O'Halloran Illuminated? . . . If the place isn't dark enough. He's right.

Proctor This place is always dark.

Logan Couldn't you find a lighter place, your grace, than this?

Proctor No place is lighter than the one I'm in.

O'Halloran To God . . .

Logan Another disaster.

O'Halloran Struck again!

Proctor *prays.*

Logan Your honour . . .

O'Halloran Has illumination been forthcoming, then?

Proctor In part.

Prays.

Logan He prays again.

Proctor I look for illumination . . .

O'Halloran Yes?

Proctor Of goals . . . of where we go . . . Of ends.

Logan (*to* **O'Halloran**) One end, illuminated, I should think, is not unlike the next.

They laugh between themselves. **Proctor** *prays.*

O'Halloran And when the end's illuminated, sir, what then?

Proctor When the goal is clear the path is straight.

Logan To God . . . but he's wrapped up in his thoughts again.

O'Halloran Ah . . . see.

Logan No, no . . .

O'Halloran He's raised his head.

Logan Is that the way . . .

O'Halloran No . . . no.

Logan It's raised again . . .

O'Halloran No . . .

Logan No . . . (*He gazes off.*)

Proctor If you wish to know the path . . . then follow me.

O'Halloran (*gazing off*) No end in view, as far as I can see.

Proctor *has risen and is moving off.*

Logan We might...

O'Halloran Follow?

Logan At a distance, then.

Proctor *has gone off.*

O'Halloran To God...

Logan *gazes off.*

O'Halloran I heard a lion roar.

Logan Not that...

O'Halloran But look.

Logan 'Tis the wildness of the man himself.

O'Halloran A sword...

Logan 'Tis fashioned from a plough.

O'Halloran A gun.

Logan He waves them by his head.

O'Halloran A crowd...

Logan His path is straight.

O'Halloran Just see the troopers drop their swords and run.

Logan A revolution.

O'Halloran The wrath of God.

Logan To Jesus!...

O'Halloran The massacre's begun.

Pause.

Logan I see no one but the man himself.

O'Halloran And all those things like stones...

Logan   Heads.

O'Halloran   And all those things that waved . . .

Logan   Hands.

O'Halloran   God . . .

Logan   The majesty . . .

O'Halloran   One voice.

A dishevelled crowd come on.

Logan   Do you travel from the place, or run?

First Traveller   We were driven out.

Second Traveller   We had no choice.

First Traveller   The land was ruled by men before.

Second Traveller   The one who rules it now is God.

First Traveller   All were equal in the land before.

Second Traveller   Now those who deal in justice suffer by the sword.

Third Traveller   Preference now is bestowed on those who seek it most.

First Traveller   He lives by intuition.

Second Traveller   A magic voice.

Third Traveller   And stands enhaloed by the sun.

First Traveller   No presence but his own commands.

O'Halloran   But here come rebels . . .

Crowd   Aye.

Third Traveller   The levellers rise again . . . they flood the land and grow, in wood and grove . . . inspired by injustice and longings for revenge.

The crowd and **Travellers** *go.*

O'Halloran   The light grows dim . . .

Logan The woods...

O'Halloran The very trees...

Logan The streams...

O'Halloran The grassy mounds.

Logan Have risen...

O'Halloran And fallen on the king...

Logan He flees...

O'Halloran And we flee...

Logan To a lighter place than this.

They go.

Dark.

Scene Eight

Light comes up.

Proctor *stands alone.*

Some distance off, the **Boatman**.

Joan *enters with* **Mathew**.

Joan I see you've found the place.

Proctor I have.

Joan Where the powerless and the unworldly meet.

Proctor I dreamed I took conviction down to hell...
cleansed and bathed its empty shell... and when I drank
I found its contents turned to blood.

Joan Boatman... shall we cross the stream?

They embark: move, stay still. The **Boatman** *poles.*

Proctor Boatman: do we cross the stream?

Boatman Aye.

Proctor   The land behind is dark.

Joan   The one in front is darker still.

Proctor   Boatman, do you know these shores?

Boatman   The stream is all I know ... its shoals, its rocks, its crevices ... its gleams ... the pattern of its light at dawn and dusk ... the rushing of its waves ... its stillness when it floods or lies, dwindling, in a summer heat ... I know the river, and the manner of the boat; that's all.

Logan and **O'Halloran** *have entered.*

Proctor   Two figures stand upon that side.

Boatman   Aye ... two travellers whom I've seen before.

O'Halloran (*calling*)   To God ... but boatman ...

Logan (*calling*)   Boatman ... take us too.

Proctor   Can't you hear them? ... Guide it back.

Boatman   The price they never have ... nor mean to pay ... They hang like leeches to the things that others have ... hands which always receive can offer nought.

Proctor   Would you take our advancement to haul the men across?

Boatman   Each must find his own, my friend ... See: the two are already drifting back: the shore holds out distractions too ...

Proctor   Do you know the other shore?

Boatman   Some say it lightens beyond its darkest fringe ... others that it presages but a thicker darkness still.

Joan   And the ones who travel back?

Boatman   No one who crosses ever comes this way again.

They disembark.

Joan See ... the boat has drifted in the stream ...

Proctor He plies the oar ...

Joan For the first time in our lives we have no turning back.

Proctor Fool: to the front ...

Joan He plunges in the dark.

Proctor The darkness thickens ...

Joan Do you hear those cries and shouts?

Proctor Are others moving in those fields that we knew before?

Joan And beyond the darkness ...

Proctor Do you see the light?

Fade.

Life Class

Late Chess

Characters

Allott
Warren
Saunders
Stella
Mathews
Brenda
Carter
Catherine
Mooney
Gillian
Abercrombie
Foley
Philips

This play was first presented at the Royal Court Theatre, London, on 9 April 1974, with the following cast:

Allott	Alan Bates
Warren	Stephen Bent
Saunders	Frank Grimes
Stella	Rosemary Martin
Mathews	Paul Kelly
Brenda	Sally Watts
Carter	David Lincoln
Catherine	Gabrielle Lloyd
Mooney	Stewart Rayner
Gillian	Brenda Cavendish
Abercrombie	Bob Peck
Foley	Brian Glover
Philips	Gerald James

Directed by Lindsay Anderson
Designed by Jocelyn Herbert

Act One

A stage.

Off-centre, stage right, is a wooden platform, some six to eight feet square, on castors.

Beside it are two metal stands, about six feet high, each equipped with two vertical flat-plane heaters. Scattered around the platform are two or three easels and several wooden 'donkeys': low, rectangular stools with an upright T-shaped bar at one end. On one, folded, is a white sheet. There are two brown hessian screens, one upstage centre, the other centre left. Upstage left is a rack with coatpegs. **Allott** *comes in stage left. In his late thirties, medium-build, he wears a duffle-coat, battered trilby hat and gloves. Blows in his hands. Thumps gloves. Shivers. Looks round. Goes over to the wall, switches on the heaters, comes back, takes off gloves, feels plates. Warms one hand, then the other: looks round, puts gloves back on. Steps back. Examines platform, head on one side. Contemplates. Returns to platform: pushes it into new position: contemplates: adjusts it slightly.*

Warren *comes in: young, well-built: overcoat and scarf. Stays at one side.*

Warren Morning, sir.

Allott Morning, Warren.

Warren *watches* **Allott** *a while adjusting platform.*

Warren . . . Nobody else here then, yet, Mr Allott.

Allott (*pays* **Warren** *no attention*) Perfectly correct.

Warren Er . . . cold.

Allott Very.

Warren Get a cup of tea.

Allott That's right.

Warren Well . . . See you.

Allott Hope so.

Warren   Yeh. (*Last look round: he goes.*)

Allott *steps back: contemplates. Goes over to heater: carries it round to the platform's new position.*

Saunders *comes in: thin, anaemic; raincoat, young.*

Saunders   Morning, sir.

Allott   Saunders.

Saunders   Need any help, sir?

Allott   Let's see. (*Takes off gloves: takes off coat.*) Could hang that up somewhere. (*Then hat.*) And that.

Saunders   Right. (*Takes them.*)

Allott   Er . . . Over there, I think . . . That's right . . . Now, then. Chalk. Pencil. (*Feels in jacket pockets: checks.*) Toilet paper . . . Seen Mr Philips, have you?

Saunders   No, sir.

Allott   Had some unfinished business there, I recollect.

Saunders   Anything else, sir?

Allott   No . . . Yes. Could chalk the platform. There's a lad. (*Hands him chalk.*)

Saunders   Right.

Allott   Shan't be a sec . . . (*Hesitates. Looks round.*) . . . Right. (*He goes.*)

Saunders *chalks off the corners of the platform on the floor.*

As he reaches the third corner, **Stella** *comes in: a model, in her twenties: she's muffled up in a heavy coat and cap: carries a shopping-bag as well as a handbag.*

Stella   Freezing. (*Shivers: goes directly to the heater.*)

Saunders   Just setting this . . .

Stella   Mr Allott here?

Saunders   He's just gone out . . .

Stella You wouldn't pop these in the cubicle, would you, love?

Saunders Yes. (*Takes the bag and handbag.*)

Stella Do my shopping on the way up. Get in early . . . Worth all the trouble . . . I'll be in the . . . Shan't be long. (*She goes.*)

Saunders *crosses to the upstage screen: takes bags behind.*

Pause.

Mathews *comes in: he's followed by* **Brenda***.*

Mathews *wears a windcheater. He's smoking.* **Brenda** *wears a coat: both are young.*

Mathews *drops his cigarette, treads it out.*

Mathews Brenda: have a ride . . .

Brenda Not likely . . . Been on there before.

Mathews *pushes the platform like a trolley: jumps on for a ride: screams out.*

Mathews Smashing.

Saunders (*coming back*) Here . . . I'm just marking that.

He takes the platform from **Mathews** *and pushes it back.*

Brenda (*to* **Saunders**) Allott here, then, is he?

Saunders Yeh.

Mathews Gone down to the bog. I bet he has . . . Spends bloody hours in there, he does.

Brenda Not the only one, I think.

Mathews Writes bloody poetry . . . Ask Warren . . . Saunders: isn't that right?

Saunders You've made a mess of this . . . I can't find the other mark.

Mathews Come on. Come on. Over here . . . that's

right. (*Helps him.*)

Brenda So cold ... (*Shivers, standing by the heater.*) Shan't do anything today ... Just look ... Can hardly hold a pencil. Dropping off. (*Holds up her hands.*)

Mathews Ought to walk here.

Brenda Walk here?

Mathews Do you good ... I walk every morning, as a matter of fact.

Brenda I've seen you.

Mathews Eyes'll drop out one day.

Brenda Tell her you're an artist, do you?

Mathews Don't need to tell her ... Can tell it at a glance.

Brenda Here. Saunders. Should have seen him. Mathews – walking: hand in hand.

Mathews What's the matter with hand in hand?

Brenda Your grubby hands ... You want to wash them.

Mathews A damn sight cleaner, love, than yours. (*Grapples with her: takes her.*)

Brenda Get off! ... Go on! ... Get *off!*

Carter (*entering*) Here. Here. Here. What's going on in here?

Carter *is small, stocky, genial: dressed in jeans and a zip-jacket, young.*

Mathews She's molesting me, Kenneth ... Ever since I came in ... Follows me around. Just look.

Having been released by **Mathews** *at* **Carter**'s *entrance,* **Brenda** *has followed him around to hit him back: now, however, she moves off.*

Carter Allott here, then, is he?

Mathews In the bog.

Carter Ay . . . is it true, then? Sits in there . . . who told me?

Mathews Warren . . .

Carter Writing verses in a book.

Mathews *laughs.*

Brenda What's the matter with writing that?

Mathews Shan't say a word . . . (*Moves off. Then:*) Should read some of it, my love.

Brenda Better than the stuff you write . . . Did you hear that Foley caught him writing on the stairs?

Carter Here . . .

Brenda On the wall.

Saunders What was that, then, Mathews?

Carter Go on, then. What did he say?

Mathews Nothing . . .

Carter Come on. Come on, then. (*To* **Brenda**.) What did he write?

Brenda Dunno . . . Had to wash it off.

Mathews Bloody obsessionalist, that man . . . Should see a doctor.

Carter Come on . . . Come on . . . When was it?

Brenda Aren't you going to tell us, Bryan?

Mathews Tell you bloody nothing . . . Mouth like a gramophone. Yak, yak, yak . . .

Brenda 'Mr Foley is feeling poorly': that's the sort of stuff he used to write.

Carter Brenda: how about it, love? (*Embraces her: sway together.*)

Saunders I've marked that platform: nobody move it.

Carter Shan't touch it. No. We shan't. We shan't. (*Hums to himself: sways with* **Brenda**.)

Mathews *picks spots on his face, standing resentfully to one side.*

Brenda (*sings*)
Have you ever ...
Asked me whether ...

Carter (*sings*)
No, I've never ...
Asked you whether.

Brenda (*sings*) I would ever ...

Carter (*sings*) You would ever ...

Brenda (*sings*) Dance the whole night long with you!

They laugh, embracing.

Catherine *comes in: late teens: dressed in a long coat and cap; carries a large straw bag. Panting, sets down her bag by a donkey: takes off cap.*

Catherine Run up all those stairs ... Do it every morning. Exercise, you know.

Mathews Could run up somewhere else with me, love. (*Guffaws.*)

Catherine *glances over: otherwise disregarding: takes off gloves.*

Brenda *has disengaged herself from* **Carter**: *she crosses over to* **Catherine**.

Brenda Did you bring it with you?

Catherine Here, then: have a look.

She gets a hat from the straw bag: tries it on for **Brenda**'s *approval.*

Mathews *crosses over to* **Carter**.

Carter Got a fag?

Mathews   Last one.

Carter   Sammy?

Saunders   Got a pipe.

Mathews   Joking.

Saunders   No, then ... (*Gets one out: puts it in his mouth.*)

Mathews   Here ... (*Takes it: tries it in his own mouth.*) How d'I look?

Carter (*ignoring* **Mathews**)   How long have you had a pipe, then, Sammy?

Saunders   A week or two ... Smoke it in the evenings.

Carter   Evenings.

Saunders   Just before I go to bed.

Mathews   Do summat else, personally, just afore I go to bed. (*Laughs, pipe between his teeth.*)

Carter *takes the pipe from him and gives it back to* **Saunders**.

Warren *comes in, dressed as before.*

Warren   Somebody's got here, then, have they? Be half of 'em away today.

Carter   Seen Allott, have you?

Warren   Yeh. Came in before ... Morning, Brenda ... Morning, Catherine.

Brenda *and* **Catherine** (*together*)   Morning, Warren.

Warren   Nice day for it. What d'you think?

Brenda   Lovely.

Warren   That your hat, then?

Brenda *has now tried it.*

Brenda   Catherine's.

Catherine   Do you like it?

Warren Dunno ... (**Catherine** *tries it.*) Suits her. (*Indicating* **Catherine**.)

Brenda Thank you. Just what I was hoping.

Mathews Here ... give us a try, then, love. (*Snatches it from her head.*)

Catherine Come here ... Give it back ... It cost a lot of money did that hat ... (*Walks after him as* **Mathews** *dances away, the hat on his head.*)

Mathews Here ... here ... How d'I look?

Brenda Give it back ...

Mathews Come and get it ... Sammy: how d'I look? (*Dances on to the platform.*)

Allott (*entering*) You the new model, are you, Mathews...? Bit over to the right. Lovely ... Lower your trousers and I think we'll be all right.

They all laugh: **Mathews** *gets down moodily from the platform.*

Catherine *takes her hat.*

Allott Spend more time getting ready for what you have to do ... turning your thoughts to higher things ... time and space ... the eternal verities ... wouldn't do you any harm. Your hat, is it, Catherine?

Catherine Yes, sir.

Allott Very nice ... (*To* **Saunders**.) Stella arrived, then, has she?

Saunders Yes, sir ... Said she wouldn't be long.

Carter Composed any poems this morning, sir?

Allott What?

Mathews Poems, sir.

The girls giggle.

Allott *pauses. Then:*

Allott   If we could have a little application ... tools of the trade ... Catherine: I should put away your hat.

Derek Mooney *and* **Gillian Stafford** *come in.* **Mooney** *has long hair.* **Gillian** *is slender.*

Mooney   Are we late, sir?

Allott   No, no, Mooney. Just in time ... Gillian.

Gillian   Morning, sir.

Allott   Looks to me as if half our members are going to be away today ... Colds. 'Flu ... Distemper ... Myxomatosis ... What do you think, Carter?

Carter   Yes, sir. Weather like this.

Allott   Seen anyone on your travels, Mooney?

Mooney   No, sir.

Allott   Except Gillian, of course.

Mooney   Yes, sir.

Allott   One day I'll find one of you two alone.

Warren   What will you do then, sir?

Allott   I shall tell – the him or her as the case may be – certain relevant facts, Warren.

Warren   What about, sir?

Allott   Facts which may well lead – the him or her as the case may be – to revise their opinion about the other ... him or her, as the case may be.

Carter   Tell us now, sir.

Brenda   What secrets have you got, sir?

Allott   Sammy: everything in order, is it?

Saunders   Yes, sir.

Mooney   What facts are they, sir?

Catherine   Gillian's dying to know, sir!

Allott It's you, Mooney, I'm worried about ... Has it ever struck you, for instance, that you've another fifty or sixty years to live?

Mooney Yes, sir.

Allott How about you, Gillian?

Gillian Yes, sir.

Allott Doesn't that come as a terrible shock?

Gillian No, sir.

Allott You'll be tired of this long-haired ninny by the time short hair comes in again.

Mooney I'll get it cut.

Allott She won't love you with it cut. Will you, Jilly?

Gillian I don't know ... I like it long.

Mooney Here, sir...!

Allott Sammy: how about these stools?

Saunders Yes, sir.

Allott Paper: pencils: ink ... (*Sees* **Mooney** *still waiting.*) Ipso facto, Mooney.

Mooney Yes, sir. (*Apprehensive: after exchanging looks with* **Gillian** *slowly goes.*)

The others wander off, except **Catherine**, *who gets a large drawing-block from her straw bag, and* **Gillian**, *who has brought her board with her.*

Stella *comes on in a dressing-gown.*

Stella Thought I'd change in the loo today. Warmer ... (*Shivers: goes to the platform: feels the heater: warms her hands.*) Gillian ... How's Derek?

Gillian All right, Stella.

Stella Wish I was young again.

Allott You are young.

Stella Really, *youthful* young.

Allott You are *youthful* young . . . as young as anybody ought to be round here . . . All these *aficionados* – myopic . . . disingenuous . . . uninspired – are images of youth no longer: pubescent excrescences on the cheeks of time.

Gillian Oh, sir!

Allott *has taken the white cloth from the donkey and crosses to the throne.*

Catherine In any case, study of natural objects isn't very popular today, sir.

Allott What?

Catherine The study of natural objects.

Allott Are you a natural object, Stella?

Stella Don't feel like one . . . Least, not natural.

Catherine I mean, anything that's real.

Allott Stella's real . . . Then again, in another sense, you could say she's quite unearthly. (**Allott** *arranges the white cloth on the throne.*)

Catherine It's more, nowadays, doing what you feel.

Allott What do you feel, Catherine?

Catherine More expressing . . . sort of . . . whatever it is.

Allott *waits.*

Catherine Well . . . sort of . . .

Allott *waits.*

Catherine I'm speaking, sort of . . . about it all in general.

Allott I see.

Brenda *comes back in with drawing-board, etc.*

Allott   I can't ask Gillian, of course ... Never known anyone feel so much with so little to show for it – except that unearthly bloody freak.

Mooney *is returning with board and paper.*

Catherine   Sir!

Brenda   She's sensitive, she is ... aren't you, love?

Gillian   Yeh.

Brenda   She feels it all the time.

Gillian   That's right.

Mathews (*re-entering*)   Here. Anybody seen my pencil?

The girls laugh.

Had it in me locker. Pack o'thieves round here ... Can't put anything down.

Brenda   No need to look in this direction.

Catherine   Accuse anybody, he would.

Gillian   Have you looked inside your pockets?

Mathews   Want to look in there, then, for me?

Gillian   Wouldn't look in there, not if they paid me.

Mathews   Not like some of the birds I know.

Stella   Here, then ... How do you want me? Standing up today, or sitting down?

Allott   Standing up, I think, to start ... Recumbent yesterday, I recollect ... Had the second years in. My God ... Licentious. To a man.

Mathews *guffaws hugely.*

Allott *circles the platform, chin in hand, contemplating the empty space.*

Stella *waits.*

Carter *and* **Warren** *have come back in.*

Warren   Saw Abercrombie on the stairs ... come in a bowler hat, he has.

Allott   What's that? (*Studies throne.*)

Warren   Come in a bowler hat, sir.

The girls laugh.

Allott   I could do with a bowler hat ... Gave hints at birthday time ... what do I get? A box of pencils.

Catherine   Artist, sir.

Allott   I have other interests, you know, as well.

Mathews   What're they, then, sir? (*He laughs, looking at the others.*)

Carter   Young ladies.

Brenda *and* **Catherine** (*together*)   Sir!

Allott   Oh, I keep my eye open, Catherine ... not very much here escapes my notice.

Gillian   I thought you were married, sir.

Allott   I am married ... I've been married in fact for a very considerable time ... In fact, the longer I stay married the more appreciative I become ...

Oh, he loved form,
And he loved beauty –
But above all else
He knew his duty.

Catherine   Oh, sir!

Allott
He called for fruit,
He called for wine:
He called for love –
But that took time.

Brenda   Go on, sir. That's super.

Allott
'I'll dream of you,' she said:
'*All life is a fantasy:*
We create illusions, call them love:'
Pray sing to me, my dove.

Carter   Anything else, sir?

Allott   No, no. That's sufficient, I think, to be going on with.

Mathews   What other interests have you got, sir?

Allott   Fishing.

Mathews   Fishing! (*Laughs.*)

Allott   You interested in fishing, Mathews?

Mathews   Not half, sir! (*Laughs.*) Things I go fishing for you don't catch in ponds. (*Laughs.*)

Allott   Where do you catch them, Mathews, if it's not too much to ask?

Warren   In his bleeding pockets.

Carter   *Dirty bugger.*

Mooney   *Dirty sod.*

Mathews   Piss off!

The others laugh.

Allott   Now, now . . . Stella here's quite shocked . . . Never knew they spoke like that, did you, Stell?

Stella   Hear some things here I'd never hear anywhere else.

Mathews   Ears like that I'm not surprised.

Allott   Here . . . Here. Now apologise for that. (*Waits.*)

Pause: **Mathews** *struggles with himself.*

Mathews   I apologise, Stella. Very much.

Stella   That's all right.

Mathews   Give you a kiss, then? Make up.

Stella   No need to go as far as that, I'm sure.

Carter   Go a damn sight farther, if he had a chance.

Allott   To your stools, men.

Guffaw from **Mathews**, **Carter**, **Warren**.

Cathy: close that door. Saunders: let's have the screen to stop the draught.

They move to the stools and easels, **Catherine** *to the entrance, stage left,* **Saunders** *to the screen, centre left: arranges it.* **Stella** *climbs on to the throne: disrobes.* **Carter** *whistles.*

Stella (*smiles, waiting to be posed*)   Enough. Enough.

Warren   Why don't you take it off more slowly?

Stella   Not for you . . . I only do that, you know, for friends.

Whistles, catcalls: **Allott** *sets the pose: standing.*

Allott   Left . . . Arm . . . More sort of . . . Right one . . .

Stella *follows his instructions.*

Allott   That's it . . . Comfortable?

Stella   Yeh.

Allott *chalks her feet: blue chalk which he takes from his pocket, marking the white sheet.*

Mathews   Watch your toes, there, darling.

Stella   Watch your something else, my love.

Mathews   Oh. Oh. Hear that . . . Everything's under control. (*Examines his flies.*) Yes . . . yes. Look. Quite nice. Quite lovely.

Carter   Dirty bugger.

Mooney   Dirty sod.

Allott   Right, then, Leonardos . . . On your marks, get set . . .

Mathews *blows raspberry.*

Allott   Go.

Laughter: fades slowly:
they start drawing. **Saunders** *comes back from setting the screen.*
Catherine *is already back.*

Each has different mannerisms:

Warren *stands, straight back, sturdy, draws with charcoal: thick, simple lines: few, much pondered.*

Saunders *uses various aids: hangs plumb-line from strut of stool to squint past: ruler to hold up at arm's length, one eye closed, to gaze at the proportions of* **Stella**: *rubber, set-square, penknife: makes numerous dots and marks, as if about to plot a map.*

Mathews *draws scruffily, ostentatiously, careless, with numerous scratching movements, scarcely looking at the model, occasionally gasping at errors, or his own performance.*

Brenda *draws in a similar fashion, but less ostentatiously. Much head-waving from side to side, with odd glances at the model, more to see if she's there, it seems, rather than by way of examination.*

Carter *stands straight-backed, like* **Warren**, *but draws a neat, well-observed, meticulous figure, unimaginative, painstaking, unengaged.*

Catherine *draws in ink: a somewhat dotted figure, like plotting out a graph: much head-waving too, with frequent – if brief – glances at* **Stella**: *the marks she makes are scarcely visible.*

Mooney *draws an idealised figure: rather like a large banana, smooth, formless, simplified almost to abstraction: studies the model conscientiously.*

Gillian *is expressionistic: enjoys drawing: puts a great deal of feeling into it, apparently; yet the result is light, sketchy, almost inconsequential.*

Allott, *after marking off the corners of the cloth on the platform with his blue chalk, walks round a moment, studying the model himself, casually, disinterested.*

Mathews   Here. Go on. Lend us it.

Saunders   Use your own.

Mathews   I haven't got one.

Allott   What is it, Marvel?

Mathews   Rubber, sir. Saunders. Won't let me have it.

Allott (*looks*)   There's nothing there.

Mathews   Is, sir. There, sir.

Allott *stoops down to* **Mathews**'s *drawing from behind* **Mathews**'s *back.*

Mathews   There.

Allott   Soot.

Mathews   No, sir! Made a mistake, sir.

Stella   Lend him it, Saunders. Last time . . . Don't want to see any rubbers after this.

All   Oh, sir!

Allott   Draw. Draw. That's all you're here to do.

Carter   What if we make a mistake, sir?

Allott   Draw round it, underneath it. Makes no difference in the end . . . *What is true will last* . . . What is real – Gillian and Mooney – is eternal.

Gillian   Oh, sir.

Mathews   Been busy already, hasn't he, Sammy?

Allott *looks across.*

Mathews   Poetical composition, sir.

Warren, **Carter**, **Brenda** *laugh.*

Allott
   Oh time is space
   And space is distance,
   Distance time

And time consuming . . .

Brenda   Sir!

Allott   Don't want to see how much, Mathews, just – how well.

Mathews   Sir.

Allott   Very nice, Catherine.

Catherine   Thank you, sir.

Allott   Fewer calculations, more intuition, Sammy: not a mathematical problem.

Saunders   Yes, sir.

Mathews   Mathematical problem to Sammy. Isn't that right.

Allott   Can't draw and talk . . . Can't demonstrate, imbibe, celebrate, Stella's peculiar beauty if you're yakketing all the time.

Abercrombie   *comes in with an electric kettle. Same age as* **Allott**: *tall, wears a polo-neck sweater, scarf with tassels, gloves, and a bowler hat.*

Abercrombie   Anybody in?

Allott   Sure.

Abercrombie   Stella.

Stella   Morning, Mr Abercrombie.

Mathews   Morning, Mr Abercrombie.

Abercrombie   Clip your ear, Warren.

Mathews   *Mathews*, sir!

Abercrombie   Clip both your ears, Mathews.

Mathews   *Sir!*

Abercrombie   Mind if I plug in, old sport?

Allott   *gestures to him to go ahead.*

Abercrombie *glances at the drawings, then at* **Stella**, *as he passes: goes to the wall: plugs in kettle.*

Abercrombie   Damn cold.

Allott   Very.

Abercrombie   Pimples. (*Indicates* **Stella**. *To* **Stella**.) Goose-pimples.

Stella   All over.

Abercrombie (*to room*)   Don't miss any out.

All   Oh, sir.

Abercrombie   How's bis?

Allott   All right.

Abercrombie   Half mine away . . . God. (*Sneezes hugely: produces handkerchief: blows.*)

Catherine   Like your hat, sir.

Abercrombie   Thank you, Catherine . . . Lends an air of distinction. (*To* **Allott**.) What d'you think?

Allott   Not seen Philips, have you?

Abercrombie   No . . . (*To* **Stella**.) Looking your splendid self, my dear.

Stella   Thank you.

Abercrombie   By God: ten years younger . . . be doing a drawing there meself.

Stella   Wonder what I'm missing.

Abercrombie   My young days, young lady, wouldn't have to wonder.

Stella   Ooooh!

Abercrombie   By God. What? . . . Might come in and do an etching . . . Not seen Foley round about?

Allott *shakes his head.*

Abercrombie   Smell his bloody pipe, but canna see the
man. (*Shivers. Slaps his hands together.*) Come cycling in the
other morning . . . found Foley parking his car by the rear
entrance to the furnace room. Says: 'This area is reserved
for artisans, Mr Abercrombie, not for members of the
teaching staff.' 'I was parking my bike here, Mr Foley, sir,'
I said. 'Bike or no bike, this is for coke, not for members
of the staff. . . ,' gesticulating then to his own automated
load of refuse and adding, 'If I leave that on the street I
get a parking ticket, so the Principal's car's excluded. All
transport apart from that has to find its own parking area.
I'd be much obliged.'

Allott   You wheeled it out.

Abercrombie   I rode it into college – left it by his door
. . . never said a word . . . made my point. Subsequently
hid it discreetly by the furnace . . . where I was this
morning when a roar – not unlike a thousand kettles
dropped at random by some insidiously careless hand –
assailed my ears . . . bob down . . . raise my head . . .
cautiously . . . find, though the symphony's subsided, the
elements as it were are still around . . . Foley . . . pink-
cheeked, perspiring – *the boot of his car wide open* – stooping
to the coke and – not lifting in huge handfuls – but
individual pieces . . . after which he wipes his hand, lowers the
boot, looks round, walks briskly – very much as if he's
accomplished a feat of unparalleled dexterity and daring –
up the steps to the college entrance.

Allott   What's he want the coke for?

Abercrombie   Fire.

Allott   In his car?

Abercrombie   At home.

Allott   He'll not get much fire with that.

Abercrombie   Suppose he picks up pieces every day . . .
after a week . . . a month . . . a year . . . the mind boggles,
Allott. He may even, in his leisure hours, run a domestic

fuel business . . . His house surrounded by veritable
mountains of first-grade coke . . .

Mathews *has had his hand up for several seconds.*

Mathews   Sir? . . .

Allott *looks up.*

Mathews   Can I be excused, sir?

Allott   What for?

Mathews (*after some hesitation, and looking round at the
others*)   I want to go, sir.

Allott   Where?

Mathews   To the bog, sir.

Allott   What do you want to do there?

Snort from **Warren**.

Mathews   Sir! I've had some medicine, sir.

Allott   What medicine?

Mathews (*hesitates. Then*)   To make me go, sir.

Allott   Go. . . ? You haven't even come.

Laughter.

Mathews   I'll have to go, sir. I've brought a note from
my mother.

Carter   He hasn't got a mother, sir.

Mathews   I've got a father.

Brenda   Different one each day.

Mathews   I'll have to go, sir!

Mooney   Dirty bugger.

Warren   Dirty sod.

Mathews   Sir!

Allott Two minutes.

Mathews Sir!

Allott Two minutes.

Mathews *Sir!*

Allott You can do all you've got to do inside two minutes.

Mathews Sir . . .

Mooney *calls to him behind his hand as he passes him to the door.*

Mathews *Piss off!* (*Goes.*)

The room subsides: the students return to work.

Stella There's a draught somewhere.

Warren That's Mathews. (*Raspberry.*)

Laughter.

Allott There's no window open, Stella . . . And the door is firmly closed. (*Glances behind screen.*) It is.

Stella I can still feel it.

Warren What's it feel like, Lovely?

Stella Nothing you might mind.

Allott Where do you feel it, Stella. . . ?

Stella Sort of . . . down my side.

Allott Which side?

Stella . . . My left side, really.

Carter That's not a draught . . . That's Sammy. (*Indicates* **Saunders**: *fixed, scrupulous examination of* **Stella**.)

Laughter.

Allott All right, I'll shift it.

Goes to one of two vertical heaters: moves it slightly, adjusting its position.

Catherine   Oh, sir!

Brenda   Oh, *sir!*

Catherine   I've drawn it, sir!

Brenda   *I*'ve drawn it, sir.

Allott   Draw it again.

Catherine   I've drawn it *there*, sir!

Allott   Draw it here, then ... How do you think Degas drew his horses ... drew his *ballet-dancers*, Catherine?

Catherine   Who, sir?

Allott   De*gas*.

Gillian   Was he a negro, sir?

Allott   No, he wasn't a negro.

Warren   Perhaps he took photographs, sir.

Allott   The moving of an electric heater isn't going to jeopardise your drawing unduly ... (*Looks.*) There's nothing there ...

Catherine   There is, sir!

Allott   Shift it.

Catherine   Sir: there'll be three of them.

Allott   Better than two ... (*To* **Abercrombie**.) Most revolutions are the result of quite arbitrary decisions taken, invariably, by people not in the least involved.

Warren   I wouldn't mind taking one or two snapshots ... Certain aspects of Stella are very photogenic.

Stella   Thank you.

Allott (*to* **Warren**)   Put away your dirty looks: get on with your dirty drawing.

Mooney   Got cramp, sir.

Allott   Where?

Mooney   Finger, sir.

Allott   Massage it.

Brenda   Ooooh, sir!

Catherine   You are awful.

Allott   Get on with it. . . ! Drive an angel to distraction
. . . Draw, for God's sake, draw!

They draw.

Your kettle finished?

Abercrombie   Boiled and re-boiled, old boy.

Allott   Saunders, haven't you sharpened that pencil
enough by now?

Saunders *goes on sharpening his pencil: he's been sharpening since*
Carter*'s reference to him.*

Brenda   He's crying, sir.

Saunders   I'm not.

Catherine   He was, sir . . .

Brenda   It's what Ken said about him, sir . . .

Gillian *has got up and gone to console* **Saunders***, arm round his*
shoulder.

Gillian   Oh, you're all right, aren't you, Sammy?

Allott   And what was Carter saying about him?

Catherine   About Stella feeling the draught, sir.

Allott   For God's sake, leave him alone, girl . . . Saunders,
put your penknife away and draw.

Gillian   I was only consoling him, sir.

Allott   You can console him after hours.

Brenda   *Sir!*

Allott   It's not a clinic, you know. It's not a haven of rest

... It's where the embryonic artist may experience –
perhaps for the very first time in his life, Brenda – the faint
flutterings of his restless spirit.

Catherine   Oh, sir!

Allott   Get on with it, for Christ's sake.

Gillian goes back reluctantly to her place.

Allott   When you've finished picking your nose, Carter,
you can go with Mr Abercrombie and ask him for a cup of
coffee. I'm parched.

Carter   Yes, sir.

Gets up promptly: waits.

Abercrombie   Right ... (*Hesitates.*) Yes. Well, after all.
That's what I came for ... Kenneth, is it?

Carter   Yes, sir.

Abercrombie   Right. We'll make Mr Allott's coffee right
away ... Two sugars ...

Allott   One.

Abercrombie   White ...

Allott   Black.

Abercrombie (*to* **Carter**)   Black. One sugar. (*Goes.*)

Carter *follows.*

Pause. Silence.

Mooney *whistles a tune contentedly to himself: low, light.*

Allott, *after calming, has begun to wander slowly round the back of
the stools, glancing at the drawings.*

Apart from the whistling, the room is silent. Then:

Allott   Musician.

Pause.

Mooney   What?

Allott Tune.

Mooney Oh.

Allott Preferably silent. (*Indicates the room.*) More creative.

Mooney Oh. (*Goes on with his drawing.*)

Allott *gazes at* **Mooney**'s *drawing. Then:*

Allott Draw that with your eyes shut?

Mooney What . . .

Allott Idealised.

Mooney What . . . ?

Allott Stella's breasts . . .

All *Ooooh!*

Allott . . . are not like water melons hanging from a tree.

Catherine Sir!

Allott They're global masses, but not conceived, as it were, Mooney, on a global scale.

Mooney Oh.

Allott A weight-lifter might find those thighs something of an encumbrance, Mooney . . . It's not a beauty contest, Mooney.

Catherine (*having come over to examine the drawing*) Oooh, sir . . . Honestly!

Allott Get back to your seat, young woman.

Catherine (*returning*) You ought to see what he's drawn, Jilly.

Brenda Better not.

Warren Cop a handful of them each evening.

Gillian Shut your mouth.

Warren Tits the size of Windsor Castle. (*Standing, peering* *over.*) Cor blimey ... get the Eiffel Tower between two o' them.

Mooney   Piss off.

Brenda (*to* **Warren**)   Upset him.

Mooney   Piss off you as well.

Allott   It's just a question ... (*Waits: they quieten, return to drawing.*) It's merely a question, Mooney of seeing each detail in relation to all the rest ... When you examine the breasts you've to bear in mind, also, the shape and volume of the head, of the chest structure beneath it, of the abdomen in general ... the proportion – the width as well as the height – of the legs: the whole contained, as it were ... (*Looks up: snigger from* **Warren**. *Silence. Return to drawing.*) ... within a single image. Unless you are constantly relating the specific to the whole, Mooney ... (**Warren** *sniggers.*) ... a work of art can never exist ... It's not merely a conscious effort; (*Gazing at the others.*) it is, if one is an artist and not merely a technician – someone disguised, that is, as an artist, going through all the motions and creating all the effects – an instinctive process ... the gift, as it were, of song ... For, after all, a bird sings in its tree (**Warren** *and* **Brenda** *snigger.*) but doesn't contemplate its song ... similarly the artist sings *his* song, but doesn't contemplate its beauty, doesn't analyse, doesn't lay it out in all its separate parts ... that is the task of the critic, the mechanic ... even of the poseur, the man masquerading as the artist ... the *manufacturer* of events who, in his twentieth-century romantic role, sees art as something accessible to all and therefore the prerogative not of the artist – but of anybody who cares to pick up a brush, a bag of cement, an acetylene welder ... anyone, in fact, who can persuade other people that what he is doing is creative ... That, after all, is the lesson we must learn, Mooney ... That's the lesson we've been convened, as it were, to celebrate ... that we are life's musicians ... its singers, and that what we sing is wholly without meaning ... it exists, merely, because it is ... The one significant distinction between the artist and the scientist, indeed, between him and all his fellow men ... What the artist does is purposeless. That's its dignity ... its beauty.

Catherine   I've run out of ink.

Allott   Well, use pencil.

Catherine   I've got some in my locker.

Allott   Well, go and get it then.

Catherine   Oh, thank you, sir. (*Goes quickly.*)

Warren   She's gone for a fag: that's what she's gone for.

Allott   Smoking in the studios, Warren, isn't allowed.

Warren   She'll smoke it in the bog.

Mooney   Mr Foley inspects the ladies' lavatories regularly: she'll not smoke anything there.

Warren   *Dirty bugger.*

Mooney   *Dirty sod.*

Allott   Commemoration of the human spirit and human hygiene often go hand in hand, Mooney.

Mooney   It wasn't me, sir. It was him.

Allott   Human hygiene and commemoration of the human spirit often go hand in hand, Warren.

Warren   Yes, sir.

Allott   Did you get that, Warren?

Warren   Yes, sir.

Allott   I'd hate you to overlook it.

Warren   Yes, sir.

Allott (*to* **Gillian**)
    Oh, love will run its course,
    Come finally to rest,
    And panting, reined in,

Stand waiting for its test.

Gillian Super, sir!

Allott Thank you, Gillian.

Catherine (*returning, breathless*) Got it, sir. (*Begins drawing immediately.*)

Allott(*to* **Warren**) Ink is what she wanted: ink is what she got.

Warren Yes, sir.

Allott A man's faith, Warren, is seldom easily come by.

Warren No, sir.

Allott The greatest harm one human being can do to another is to seek to disillusion him ... some people take longer, for instance, to fill their pens than others.

Warren Yes sir.

Allott And some, of course, never need to fill their pens at all.

Warren No, sir.

Mooney *and* **Brenda** *snigger.*

Allott Is that a mystery figure, Brenda? ... Have we – at the end of the day – to decide what it is, where it came from, and who its antecedents are?

Brenda No, sir.

Allott Unformed. Wouldn't you say that's a reasonable assessment, Brenda?

Brenda No, sir.

Allott What Mooney's has got a superabundance of, yours has got none at all.

Catherine It's different for a girl, sir.

Allott How do you mean?

Catherine   Well, sir . . .

Brenda   Drawing breasts, sir.

Gillian   Yeh.

Catherine   It's different for a girl.

Brenda   If we'd got a feller to draw it'd be different, sir.

Catherine   We could get going with a feller, sir.

Warren   Hang one on him three feet long.

Mooney   *Dirty bugger.*

Warren   *Dirty sod.*

Allott   Warren – *if* you're doing anything at all, that is – it's of far greater interest to me than any of these diverting comments you feel constrained to make from time to time. (*Waits.*) Get on with it.

Warren   It's sexual discrimination, sir.

Allott   There's no sexual discrimination here . . . Art is above sex . . . and it's above politics, too. That's to say, it absorbs sex, and it absorbs politics.

Brenda   Why're we always drawing women, then?

Allott   You're not always drawing women.

Gillian   We are in here.

Catherine   That's sexual discrimination. That's what I mean.

Allott   We had a man once. I remember distinctly.

Warren   Gave 'em all a shock, sir . . . Shoulda seen it. Almost to his knee-caps, sir.

Gillian   S'only nature.

Catherine   Yeh. It's only nature.

Brenda   That's what I mean . . . Just once.

Allott   We're not here to seek sexual stimulation,

Catherine. We're here to peruse a beautiful and seemingly mysterious object, and to set it down – curiously – as objectively as we can.

Brenda   It's alus a woman, sir.

Saunders   Women have always been the subject of the very greatest art.

Pause: they look at **Saunders**.

Because all the greatest artists, you see, have always been men.

Gillian   We know why, don't we, Sammy?

Allott   I don't know why. Have you some information on the subject you've been keeping back from us, Jilly?

Gillian   They like contemplating their human slaves.

Warren   What slaves?

Saunders   Who's a slave?

Gillian   Us. We're slaves.

Mooney   Who keeps you in slavery?

Gillian   You do.

Mooney   Me?

Catherine   *Men.*

Warren   Bollocks.

Gillian   That's a man's answer to everything . . . *Bollocks.*

Mooney   I don't like women swearing . . . I've told you that before.

Gillian   Piss off!

Brenda   Ooooh, Jilly!

Warren   They're a pain in the arse, sir. They are, honestly.

Saunders   If women wanted to be artists they've more

time than anybody else.

Brenda Rubbish . . .

Catherine Bollocks!

The girls laugh.

Warren Cor blimey . . . sat on their backsides all day at home . . . if they wanted to paint bloody pictures they'd find the time, don't worry.

Gillian That's what you know. That's all you think.

Warren Cor blimey . . . bored out of their minds, middle-class women.

Saunders Look at the rich, well-to-do women in the nineteenth century.

Warren Tell me they haven't had the opportunity or the time . . .

Saunders As for the men . . .

Warren Work their bollocks off feeding a bloody family, *then* come home and create a work of art . . . you don't know when you're well off.

Brenda Piss off.

Warren You piss off.

Catherine You piss off.

Warren And *you* piss off.

Allott Discussions of this sort invariably serve a useful function, clarifying the issues, setting them, if anything, in a wider context, removing the edge of personal, not to say sexual, vindictiveness . . .

Warren (*to* **Brenda**) Get this up your nose you'd piss off all right.

Brenda Get this somewhere else and you'd piss off all right.

Allott The education of the working class of course is still something of an anomaly.

Warren (*to* **Brenda**) Bollocks!

Brenda Bollocks.

Warren You haven't got no bollocks.

Brenda Neither have you!

Laughter from the girls.

Allott You could say that women have never had the *consciousness* to become artists – there are exceptions but I mean as a general rule.

Warren Yeh, but, sir . . .

Saunders I mean, don't you think that it would be extraordinary, Mr Allott, that something that has been denied women for so long should have taken all this time to emerge – I mean, their natural but frustrated capacity to be great thinkers, great composers, great artists, great poets . . . great originators of thought and feeling? It seems humanly impossible that if this is an intrinsic part of the female temperament it should never have shown itself in any of these forms.

Catherine Yeh . . . but that's the point, i'n it? In women it's been made *unnatural*.

Warren Piss off.

Catherine You piss off!

Brenda Whose side are you on, sir?

Allott Nobody's. That's to say, I'm accepting that anything is possible, but that for now, at this minute, Stella is standing there, in all her pristine glory . . .

Stella I've got pins and needles.

Allott Whether women have been the object – or even the subject – of men's abuse, she is – and I insist that you still see her as – a human being. And it's as a human being you'll draw her, and it's as a human being you'll record your impressions of her ... insufferable to look at as some of those impressions well may be.

Stella   Can I have a rest?

Allott   No.

Gillian   Sir!

Allott   She's always trying to get round me.

Catherine   Sir!

Allott   If she's really got pins and needles she'd have collapsed already. Can you feel a draught?

Stella   No.

Allott   Right, then.

Mathews (*entering*)   Those bogs want cleaning out.

Laughter.

Gillian   After you've been in, especially.

Mathews   *Afore* I went in ... That caretaker never goes in there. Sweeps to the bloody door then stops.

Warren   What are you, Mathews, man or woman?

Mathews   If you've two minutes to step outside I'll show you.

Warren   I mean in the political contest between the sexes, Bryan. Are you a man or are you a woman?

Mathews   I'm a woman. I'm on the woman's side in everything.

Mooney   Front and back, an' all: it makes no difference to Mathews.

Mathews (*makes a fist*)   You'll get this under your fucking nose.

Brenda   How did your medicine work, then? Long and easy?

Mathews   And up yours . . . I'm not above using this, you know.

Warren   But slowly. Each evening, tha knows, afore he goes to bed.

Laughter from the girls.

Mathews   Piss off.

Catherine, **Gillian** *and* **Brenda** (*together*)   *Piss off!* (*They laugh.*)

Allott   Coffee time, nearly. (*Examines his watch: winds it.*)

Brenda   Aren't you going to do any drawing, sir?

Allott   I might . . . I might. (*Examines watch again.*) This time of the day the mind unfolds . . . my time of life, however, Brenda, inspiration often falters.

Catherine   What about us, then, sir?

Allott   I was coming to you, Catherine, as a matter of fact . . . These invisible compositions . . . You look (*Indicates* **Stella**.) . . . Examine . . . Set down . . . But I'm damned if I can find a mark.

Catherine   There, sir.

Allott   Where. . . ?

Catherine   Head . . . arms . . . legs . . . feet.

Allott   What's that?

Catherine   Her head, sir.

Allott   It's a piece of fluff. (*Brushes it off with his hand.*) No it's not.

Catherine   It's her head, sir.

Allott   What's this?

Catherine   Her breast, sir.

Warren, **Mathews** *and* **Mooney** (*together*)   *Ooooh!*

Allott   Where's the other one?

Warren   She hasn't got one.

Laughter.

Catherine   I haven't done it, sir.

Allott   There are two of these objects ... perhaps you haven't noticed. And good grief. This other bit of fluff ...

Catherine   I was pinpointing the principal masses, sir.

Allott   You've been stabbing them to death. Just look at this.

Mathews, *rising, has leaned over to look.*

Mathews   One tit, one cunt: that's all she's got.

Allott (*straightens: surveys* **Mathews** *for a moment. Then*)   I know your personality hasn't a great deal to recommend it, Mathews; but what little charm it does possess is scarcely enhanced by a remark like that ... If you could just concentrate on the job in hand.

Warren   He hasn't got it in hand, sir; that's his trouble.

Allott   The object, Mathews. The thing you see before you ... I take it that's your latest design for a coal-mine, Warren.

Warren   Sir?

Allott   Is there a human being lying somewhere under that?

Warren   It's very difficult to concentrate here, sir.

Allott   Michelangelo lay on his back all day to paint the Sistine ceiling ... he drew on his inner resources, Warren ... brought them up from deep inside.

Mathews *belches.*

Allott   Unaided, even, by patent laxative. (*Returns to* **Catherine**.) The problem, Catherine ... isn't to pinpoint ... nor even to isolate ... it's to incorporate everything that is happening out there into a single homogeneous whole.

Catherine (*gazing at* **Stella**) There's nothing happening, sir.

Allott There's a great deal happening ... Not in any obvious way ... nevertheless several momentous events are actually taking place out there ... subtly, quietly, not overtly ... but in the way that artistic events *do* take place ... in the great reaches of the mind ... the way the leg, for instance, articulates with the hip, the shoulders with the thorax; the way the feet display the weight ... the hands subtended at the end of either arm ... these are the wonders of creation, Catherine ... Is your pen absolutely full? (*Has taken it to indicate the parts of the drawing to her: no mark. Shakes it down violently.*)

Catherine Sir: you've blotted!

Allott Blots are indicative of industry, Catherine. Of energy. Passion. Draw round it. (*Rises, handing the pen to her.*)

Warren Could make it into your pubic, Cathy.

Catherine Piss off.

Warren You piss off as well.

Carter (*entering with cup and saucer*) Coffee up, sir.

Allott Not before time.

Brenda Rest, sir?

Allott The model is there, Brenda, for your edification. She's not a motif. Your glances in her direction – few and far between – are to reassure yourself she's still in the room. She is there to be examined ... If only at a distance, Carter.

Stella *has whispered to* **Carter**, '*Any for me?*'; *he's gone nearer to answer.*

Allott ... If only at a distance, Carter.

Carter   I didn't say anything, sir.

Allott   Coffee cold?

Carter   No, sir. It's just been made.

Allott   I don't want to find anything in the saucer.

Carter   No, sir.

Allott   Hold it straight. (*To* **Mathews**.) I'm not sure what comment I can make on Mathews' ... An advertisement, perhaps, for rubber tyres ... (*Twists his head.*) Or the effect of too much alcohol on the human brain ... (*Twists his head again.*) Burnt porridge, emerging through a Scotch mist ... at three, perhaps three-thirty of a winter's morn ...

Mathews   I've not had time to get started, sir.

Allott   That's what I mean ... The whole process, Mathews, has not begun: mass before beauty, excrescence before edification ... salaciousness before refinement ... Has anyone here seen Mr Philips?

Brenda   No, sir.

Gillian   No, sir.

Warren   No, sir.

Mathews   Got something on, then, have you?

Allott   What?

Mathews *makes the sound of a galloping horse, clicking his tongue against his teeth – and holding a pair of invisible reins, urgently, in his hands.*

Allott   You still taking that medicine, Mathews?

Mathews   No, sir.

Allott   Better get downstairs ... and take another dose. *Rest!*

Laughter: scramble for the door.

Stella *descends, stretching.*

Brenda   How long we got, sir?

Allott   As long as I tell you.

Warren   Watch it, Stella. (*Grapples with her.*)

Stella   Get off, you filthy-minded beast.

Mathews *blows raspberry: they all go, but for* **Saunders***: after getting up slowly, even reluctantly, he wanders round the drawings, examining.*

Allott   Going for a cup of tea, Samuel?

Saunders   Yes, sir ... (*Casual.*) Stella? You going?

Stella   I'll be along in a minute, love ... My back ... Can you see anything on it? (*Turns it to* **Allott**.)

Allott   Here?

Stella   No ...

Allott   Here?

Stella   Here ...

Allott   What sort of thing?

Stella   Knocked it ... when I got up it was terribly stiff ... I'll be along in a jiffy, Sammy.

Saunders (*who's been waiting*)   Oh ... all right. (*Glances at her: goes.*)

Stella   Been measuring me again.

Allott   Who?

Stella   Sammy ... Look at all these plumb-lines ... Anybody'd think he was going to reconstruct me ... build me in concrete somewhere else.

Allott   Your statistics are of immeasurable significance to him, Stella ... I can't see anything at all.

Stella   You coming, are you? (*Puts on her dressing-gown.*)

Catherine *has come back in.*

Allott   No, no. I'll drink it here.

Stella   See you. (*Goes.*)

Catherine *has gone to throne, sat down with her straw bag: gets out flask, sandwiches: pours tea.*

Allott *watches her. Then:*

Allott   Cucumber?

Catherine   Lettuce.

Allott   Looks just like cucumber from over here.

Catherine   Lettuce.

Allott   Don't you eat anything else?

Catherine   Haven't got time.

Allott   My wife is coming up today.

Catherine   Is she, sir? What for?

Allott   We've been separated, you know, for some considerable time. She's coming, I suspect, to give me news of a very significant nature ... or, in the terminology of the employment exchange, my cards.

Catherine   Oh, I'm sorry, sir.

Allott   One of those things. The artist, after all, has no real life outside his work. Whenever he attempts it, the results, Catherine, leave – to say the very least of it – a great deal to be desired ... Refreshing.

Catherine   Yes, sir?

Allott   Cucumber ... Don't you find it refreshing?

Catherine   Have one, sir, if you want.

Allott   No. No ... I couldn't eat a thing.

Catherine   What sort of pictures do you paint, sir?

Allott   I don't.

Catherine   Do you do sculpture, then?

Allott No. (*Shakes his head.*)

Catherine What do you do, then, sir?

Allott It's my opinion that painting and sculpture, and all the traditional forms of expression in the plastic arts, have had their day, Catherine ... It's my opinion that the artist has been driven back – or driven on, to look at it in a positive way – to creating his works, as it were, in public.

Catherine In public, sir?

Allott Just as Courbet or Modigliani, or the great Dutch masters ... created their work out of everyday things, so the contemporary artist creates his work out of the experience – the events as well as the objects – with which he's surrounded in his day-to-day existence ... for instance, our meeting here today ... the feelings and intuitions expressed by all of us inside this room ... are in effect the creation – the re-creation – of the artist ... to the extent that they are controlled, manipulated, postulated, processed, defined, sifted, refined ...

Catherine Who by, sir?

Allott Well, for want a better word – by me.

Pause.

Catherine Oh.

Foley (*entering*) Has somebody been bloody well smoking in here?

Foley *is a bluff, red-faced man, an embryonic wrestler in physique: about fifty to fifty-five.*

Allott (*standing immediately*) No.

Foley (*gazing round. Then*) Who?

Catherine (*rising abruptly*) Catherine, sir.

Foley Pipe tobacco ... they can't even be honest about it and smoke a cigarette ... Think it'll get wafted up with my own ... Think, you know, that a smoker can't smell his own tobacco. I'm different in that respect ... Who?

Catherine   Catherine, sir.

Foley   What?

Catherine   Smith, sir.

Foley   Any relation to Walter Smith?

Catherine   No, sir.

Foley   Walter Smith's a very fine window cleaner. Cleans my windows a treat. Where's everybody gone?

Allott   Rest.

Foley   What's this? (**Warren**'s *drawing*.)

Allott   He's breaking it down, I believe ... into its individual masses.

Foley   Crushing it to bloody death, it seems to me. (*Turns the drawing upside down.*) The Black Hole of Calcutta ... See it? ... All those figures? ... And that man trying to claw his way towards the light ...

Allott   Yes.

Foley   I should suggest he starts on it upside down.

Allott   Yes.

Foley   What's this...? (*Peers closely at* **Catherine**'s.)

Allott   That's Catherine's, as a matter of fact.

Foley   Sat here all morning doing nowt, then.

Allott   There are one or two marks ... indicative of the principal masses.

Foley   T'only thing I can see is a bloody blot ... Doesn't take long to draw a blot ... This the pen you use, then, is it? ... You don't want to use ought automatic when you turn to art ... automatic pens are out ... plastic paraphernalia that no artist of any note has any time for ... Sithee (*To* **Allott**.): when you set a pose, you want to

set a teaser ... summat'll stretch em out ... arm up here
... leg out ... hip thrust in opposite direction (*Shows him.*)
... All this straight up and down nonsense, I reckon nowt
to that ... The model doesn't smoke, then, does she?

Allott   I'm not sure.

Foley (*looks behind screen*)   Where's her undies?

Allott   She changes in the ladies ... warmer.

Foley   No relation to Gordon Smith?

Catherine   No, sir.

Foley   Seen Philips, have you? (*Going.*)

Allott   I was looking for him myself.

Foley   Think on: arm up, leg out. Get summat classical,
tha knows. (*Goes.*)

Catherine *sighs. Sits down.*

Allott *sits too, after a moment.*

Catherine   I didn't see you doing much controlling there,
sir.

Allott   I wouldn't agree with you entirely, Catherine ...
Silence can guide, you know, as well as absorb.

Catherine   I don't think anyone guides Mr Foley.

Allott   There are certain ungovernables in life, but even
they can be incorporated into a general pattern – into a
single, coherent whole ... other things, of course, don't
have to be guided.

Catherine   Such as, sir?

Allott   Natural impulses. Feeling creates its own form,
form its own feeling.

Catherine   I'm not sure what you mean there, sir.

Allott   Who can distinguish between the feeling, for
instance, that informs a shape, and the shape itself? The

one is a natural concomitant of the other ...
indistinguishable. Inseparable.

Waits.

Then again, in personal feelings who's to say that what one
feels for an individual can ever be separated from how they
look, or are, or indeed, as the phrase goes, have their
being? I have my feelings about you, Catherine, and I
associate them, irretrievably, with your appearance – how
you walk, and speak ... is that your hat?

Catherine   I brought it this morning to show to Brenda.

Allott   It's very becoming ...

Catherine *puts it on, unselfconscious.*

Allott *watches.*

Allott   Really ...

Catherine   Do you like it?

Allott   It's very beautiful ...

Catherine *turns her head.*

Allott   What could be simpler ... I really think ... well.
It's very charming.

Pause.

Warren *puts his head round the screen from the door.*

Warren   Foley's looking for a smoker ... In the women's
bogs. Asked me if there was anyone I knew who smoked a
pipe.

Catherine   He does.

Warren   'You, sir.' That's what I said. *He* said: 'None of
your bloody cheek, Carter, or I'll clip you round the head.'
I said, 'My name's Warren, sir.' He said, 'Well, I'll clip
Warren round the head,' and added, after a moment's
reflection, *threateningly*, 'You can tell him that from me.' (*To*
Catherine.) Was Saunders crying?

Catherine Course he was . . .

Warren Poorly, is he?

Catherine He's in love with Stella.

Warren Can't be.

Catherine Can't see why not.

Allott Artists have frequently been known to fall in love with the subject of their art.

Warren Not Saunders. He can't look at a tit without getting out a ruler.

Allott Perhaps it's the wrong instrument, but the instinct, I'm sure, is still the same.

Warren Who'd have believed it?

Catherine I'll go and put my hat in the locker. It might get damaged up here.

Warren Might get nicked. (*Gesturing off.*)

Catherine The women you can trust here, Warren. (*Goes.*)

Warren *wanders aimlessly round the drawings. Then:*

Warren You go in for all this art, then, sir?

Allott It's a job . . .

Warren Doesn't seem real, somehow.

Allott We all sail, to some extent, under false colours, Warren . . . I mean, you may not see yourself as an artist . . . I may not see myself as a teacher . . . No one of any consequence paints the human figure, for instance, any more . . . it's not even a discipline because, if you presented me with a straight line and told me that's what you saw – under the absurd licence of modern illusionism – I'd have to accept it. Stella earns her living; I earn my living . . . you earn your living – a mere pittance, I agree – one of the world's exploited . . . but between us, we convene . . .

celebrate . . . initiate . . . an event, which, for me, is the very antithesis of what *you* term reality . . . namely we embody, synthesise, evoke, a work, which, whether we are aware of it or not, is taking place around us . . . (*Indicates* **Saunders**' *entrance.*) all the time.

Warren *watches* **Saunders**, *who makes no gesture to them: he crosses to the throne, sits there, on the edge, away from them. Then:*

Warren All right, Sammy?

Saunders Yeh.

Warren (*looking at* **Saunders**' *drawing*) Not got much done for a morning.

Saunders No.

Warren Still . . . Plenty of time yet, Sam.

Saunders Yeh.

Carter *enters: eyes on* **Saunders**: *evidently been following him outside. He's followed in by* **Mathews**, *eyes on* **Saunders** *too.*

Carter How's Sammy?

Saunders All right.

Mathews Cleared up, has it?

Saunders What?

Mathews Eye . . .

Saunders Yeh.

Mathews Lot o' dust . . . (*Wafts round.*) . . . can see it circling . . . (*Gazes up, following it with finger.*) Ooh! (*Clutches his eye.*)

Warren What's all this?

Carter Tell you later.

Mathews (*to* **Warren**) S-a-m invited Stella out tonight.

Saunders What's Stella say?

Mathews *and* **Carter** (*together*) Piss off! (*They laugh.*)

Saunders *gets up: finds nowhere to go: goes to donkey: strips sheet of paper from his board. Sits.*

Warren Mr Foley's been looking for a pipe-smoker, Sammy.

Saunders Has he?

Warren Got his suspicions.

Mathews Came out of the women's bog.

Carter Dirty bugger . . .

Mathews Dirty sod!

Warren She was only an artist's daughter . . .

Mathews But she knew where to draw the line.

Laughter.

Carter Going, sir?

Allott *has made a move for the door.*

Allott Yes . . . I shan't be a moment . . . Paper . . . Pen . . . (*Feels in his pockets.*) Ah, yes. Here we are. (*Goes.*)

Carter Diarrhoea!

Warren Constipation!

Mathews Poetry coming on!

They laugh.

Warren Why's he teach in this pissed-off dump?

Saunders Van Gogh couldn't even get a job.

Mathews Who's Van Gogh?

Laughter.

Saunders Don't judge people by appearances; that's all, Warren.

Carter That's your considered opinion is it, Sammy?

Saunders It's not considered. It's just a simple fact of life.

Mathews You know a lot about life then, Sammy.

Saunders I don't know much at all, as a matter of fact. I know something about Mr Allott, though.

Carter What?

Saunders That he's sincere in his beliefs.

Warren Is he?

Saunders *doesn't answer.*

Mathews What beliefs are those, when they're all at home?

Saunders Perhaps there isn't a role left for the artist ... perhaps, in an egalitarian society – so-called – an artist is a liability ... after all, he's an individual: he tells you by his gift alone that all people can't be equal ... why should one person have a beautiful voice if we can't all have it...? That's what it's coming to ... That's an opinion, however, not a fact of life.

Carter Why go on measuring up all these beautiful women, Sammy?

Saunders There's something dispassionate in human nature ... that's what I think ... something really dispassionate that nothing – no amount of pernicious and cruel experience – can ever destroy. That's what I believe in ... I think a time will come when people will be interested in what was dispassionate at a time like this ... when everything was dictated to by so much fashion ... by fashion and techniques.

Warren You draw like a machine: what you worrying about?

Saunders I use a bit of string, and a stone. If I can't measure what I see how can I relate it?

Warren Silly prick.

Carter   He talks like Allott.

Warren   He looks like Allott.

Mathews   He smells like Allott.

Carter, **Warren** and **Mathews** (*together*)   *He is Allott!* (*They laugh.*)

Brenda *comes in.*

Brenda   Have we started?

Carter   Not yet, my darling. (*Embraces her.*)

Brenda   Get off ... (*Stays in his embrace, however.*) That coffee does terrible things to your stomach.

Mathews   Come a bit closer and I might do something better.

Brenda   Piss off. (*Sways with* **Carter** *in embrace.*)

Warren   I don't think women should swear, as a matter of fact.

Mathews   Neither do I.

Brenda   Why not?

Warren   I'll tell you why ... I've never heard *one* who can do it with conviction.

Brenda   Fuck off.

Warren (*to* **Carter**)   There's a first time, you see, for everything.

Catherine *enters, gasping.*

Catherine   Have we started?

Brenda   No, love. (*Kissing* **Carter**, *in whose arms she still sways.*)

Catherine   Once up and down the stairs ... (*Collapses on donkey.*)

Warren   Why d'you do it, Catherine?

Catherine   Get varicose veins, you know, with sitting.

Mathews   I could give you all the exercise you want.

Catherine   So I've heard.

Warren   Follows you up and down, he does.

Carter   Stairs . . .

Warren   Likes the colour of your knickers.

Catherine   That's as close as he'll ever get.

Mathews   I think women ought to wear trousers, as a matter of fact.

Brenda   Why?

Carter *has already released her.*

Mathews   Look silly wearing skirts. Men don't show off their underwear, do they?

Brenda   Not your dirty, filthy, bloody stuff.

Mathews   Piss off.

Warren   Get your hand in easier, Bryan. (*Gropes* **Brenda**.)

Mathews   Yeh . . . Hadn't thought of that!

Brenda   Piss off.

Warren   Piss off yourself . . . (*Raspberry.*)

Mathews *joins* **Warren** *with* **Brenda**: *they fight.* **Philips** *enters.*

Philips (*briskly*)   Morning, boys . . . Mr Allott about, then, is he? . . . Morning, ladies.

Philips *is a small, dapper, military figure, stiff, between forty and fifty: he bows to the two girls as the fighting subsides.*

Warren   He's popped out for a moment, Mr Philips.

Philips   By God, rest time, is it?

Carter   Yes, sir.

Mathews   Was there any message in particular you wanted passing on, sir?

Philips (*crossing to throne and heaters*)   Lovely and warm in here . . . Warmest room in the building.

Warren   We're about to start any minute, sir.

Philips   I'll hang on. I'll hang on. (*Warms his hands at the heater.*) By God: tempted to become a model, you know, myself.

Carter   Is it true at one time, sir, you were an amateur boxer? (*Glancing at the others.*)

Philips   That's quite correct.

Carter   Lightweight, sir?

Philips   Oh, one of the lightweight categories, you can be sure of that . . .

Warren   Still in good shape, sir.

Philips   I could give a round or two to some of these youngsters nowadays . . . Two days of roadwork and they want to turn professional . . . By God, some of the best boxers of the day, you know, were amateur . . . never stepped inside a professional ring. Knew what the business was all about and had their priorities in the proper order. The moment sport and money mix, the former – you can take it from me – goes out of the window.

Stella (*entering*)   Time is it?

Philips   My God, and come out fighting! (*Dances forward, fists ready: laughs.*)

Stella   Oh, Mr Philips . . .

Philips   Up on your throne, young lady. Give it all you've got . . . Come on, come on, there. Mr Allott can't be far away, I can tell you that.

They go slowly to their respective easels and donkeys.

Saunders, *who has been sharpening his pencil since his last dialogue, has attached a fresh sheet of paper to his drawing-board.*

Stella *mounts the platform.*

Philips   Few masterpieces I can see already on the way ... Might turn that into a lithograph, Carter ... one or two nice textures there ...

Carter   That's Warren's.

Philips   All true art is impersonal. Who said that?

Mathews   Mr Allott, sir.

Philips (*pause. Then*)   That's quite correct.

Stella   Well ... Are you ready?

Warren   Ready.

Mathews   Ready.

Carter   Ready.

Stella   For *drawing*.

Warren   Mr Philips is dying for a look ...

Philips   Oh, I've seen plenty of models in my time, I can tell you that ... Those of us in the Design Department aren't that far removed from life ... Now, what's the pose...? Chalk marks all correct?

Philips *stands by the throne.*

Stella *removes her robe.*

Philips *gazes at her.*

Philips   Left ... more left ... (*Glances at one of the drawings.*) Right hand ... That's correct ... (*Looks round.*) Everyone satisfied?

Warren   If you are, sir.

Philips   Oh, I'm satisfied ... I'm satisfied well enough ... Catherine, my dear?

Catherine   Yes, sir.

Philips   Brenda?

Brenda   Yes, sir.

They all begin.

They work in silence: gradually, one by one, heads turn and gaze at **Saunders** *who, solemnly, has begun his measuring out and his careful drawing. After a while the whole room's attention is on him, even finally* **Stella** *herself, who, without moving her body, turns her head and looks.*

Saunders, *aware of her gaze, looks up.*

Philips, *who has been inspecting the girls' drawings from behind their backs, looks up too.*

Philips   Is anything the matter?

Warren   No, sir.

Mathews   No, sir.

Carter   No, sir.

Brenda   No, sir.

Catherine   No, sir.

Philips   Well, then ... get on with it.

They begin again. After a while the heads begin to turn again: finally they all gaze at **Saunders**.

Saunders, *drawing, becomes aware of their fresh scrutiny. After a moment's hesitation he gets up: takes up his plumb-line, his various pieces, his board, his paper.*

Gillian *and* **Mooney** *come in as* **Saunders** *leaves. He brushes past them, goes.*

Mooney   What's up with Sammy, then?

Carter   Love-sick.

Warren   Silly pillock.

Mathews *blows raspberry.*

Gillian Hello, Mr Philips.

Mooney Filling in. . . ?

Philips Temporary absence of Mr Allott . . . And which is your drawing, my dear?

Gillian This one.

Philips Delicate . . . very delicate. (*Examines it, then indicates* **Stella**.) You'll notice . . . (*Crosses to* **Stella**.) the thigh . . . (*Runs his hand along it.*) is relaxed when the weight is on the other foot . . . it's suspended from the pelvis . . . here . . . at a lower point than where – because it's taking the weight – it's *inserted* on the other side . . . (*Demonstrates with both hands.*)

Gillian Yes.

Philips The hips, therefore, represent something of an acute angle, subtended from the horizontal.

Warren He's not going to grope her, is he?

Philips Have I made it clear?

Gillian Yes, sir.

Philips *moves back to the drawing: walks around the rear of the students: leans over one or two boys.*

Philips (*to* **Carter**) More . . . That's better . . . (*Points it out on the paper. Moves on. To* **Warren**.) Clearer . . . clearer . . . A good clean line . . . (*To* **Mathews**, *after a quick perusal and passing on.*) That's coming on . . .

Work in silence for a while.

In silence **Allott** *enters: unnatural: looks round. Pause. Then:*

Allott Where's Saunders, then?

Carter Love-sick, sir.

Philips Temporarily absented . . . One or two nice effects . . . (*Indicates students' work.*)

Allott Blue Moon came up at Kempton.

Philips Do you want it in tens or fives?

Allott It always feels much better in shillings. (*Holds out his hand.*)

Philips *sorts coins: hands them over.*

Allott Looked for you all over this morning.

Philips Dear boy: I've only just arrived.

Allott You don't understand, Philips. This is the first time I've ever won.

Philips Incredible, old boy ... No, no. really. (*Sorts last coin: hands it over.*)

Allott (*gazing up*) Somewhere, in that indefinable miasma we call life, there's some creature looking down ... 'Allott,' it said. 'Allott ... Let Allott win the four-fifteen.'

Philips Nearly the three o'clock as well.

Allott That was a different matter entirely.

Philips I said go for a place, old boy.

Allott I just felt that fate had bigger things in store.

Philips It had. It had.

Allott (*gazes at the coins in his hand. Then*) I'd almost given up hope, Philips.

Philips Don't give up hope, old boy ... After all, what're we in this business for ... No. This. (*Indicates the model, room.*)

Allott Ah ... Yes.

Philips Posterity, old son. If they don't see it now they'll see it later. We're building up an enormous credit ... (*Gestures aimlessly overhead.*) somewhere ... You with your ... events ... me with my designs ... book-jackets, posters ... Letraset ... singular embodiments of the age we live in.

Allott   Sold anything lately?

Philips (*shakes his head*) ... You?

Allott   How do you sell an event that no one will admit is taking place?

Philips   Have to go back to painting, old boy.

Allott   I know when I'm licked, Philips. It's all or nothing ... avant-garde or bust.

Philips   Old boy ...

Allott   It's not important.

Philips   Don't give up ... that's the message ... that's the message that comes down to us from Rembrandt ... from Cézanne ... from all that countless host who sank their existences in art ...

Allott   Don't you get the feeling at times that it's a substitute for living?

Philips   This *is* life ... Dear boy ... just look around you ... the youth of today ... the human body (*Indicates* **Stella**.) ... what more could one desire?

Allott   You're right.

Philips   How much do you want on?

Allott   I haven't looked at a paper yet ... I haven't got over the shock of this one ... I even told my wife ... on the phone, you know ... we've been separated now for several months ... '25p?' she said. 'You're going crazy.' And the fact of the matter is, at times, I really think I am.

Philips   Baudelaire ... Dostoevsky ... Nietzsche ... you have to bear them all in mind ... men who teetered on the very brink of human existence and had the privilege ... the temerity, even – to gaze right over the edge ...

Allott   I've gazed over the edge, Philips, long enough ... it's the staying there that worries me ... I'm beginning to think I'll never get back ... How does one live as a revolutionary, Philips, when no one admits there's a revolution there?

Philips Prophet in his own country, old boy ... Think of Christ.

Allott I think of nothing else ... I'm even beginning to think, Philips, that it's not my duty to resurrect mankind.

Philips Stranger things have happened, boy ... Lucky Horseshoe, two-fifteen ... obvious choice ... But then Blue Moon stuck out a mile.

Allott How much?

Philips Can get you eight to one, old boy.

Allott (*counting his money*) 10p ... leaves me with 15.

Philips That's the spirit ... (*Takes the money.*) Anything worth doing ... (*To* **Catherine** *as he leaves.*) Firmer! Firmer! ... (*To* **Allott**.) Commit yourself: that's all it means. (*Goes.*)

Allott *stands there for a while; gazes before him, abstracted. Then:*

Allott All right ... Everyone?

Brenda Yes, sir.

Catherine Yes, sir.

Gillian Yes, sir.

Mooney Yes, sir.

Warren Yes, sir.

Allott Good ...

Mathews *Yes, sir!*

Allott Good ... good. That's the spirit ... Labor Ipse Voluptas Est.

Warren Rest, sir?

Allott No, no ... Just carry on.

Fade.

Act Two

Scene One

Stage empty. Light faint.

Abercrombie *comes on, dressed in sweater, scarf, plimsolls, shorts. Carries a racquet.*

Silence.

Abercrombie I say ... (*Returns to screen: a moment later lights come on. Comes back.*) Anyone for squash?

Groans from behind model's screen.

Goes to screen: looks behind.

I'm terribly sorry ...

Stella (*heard, stretching*) Ooooh...!

Abercrombie Fancy a knock-up?

Stella (*heard*) No thanks.

Abercrombie Looks like thunder. (*Indicates off.*)

Stella (*emerging in dressing-gown*) I was sleeping ... (*Stretches.*) It's so much quieter lying in here.

Abercrombie (*ducking down and gazing up*) Or snow ...

Stella Play that often?

Abercrombie Lunch times ... winter mostly. Summer – tennis.

Stella Oh ... (*Stretches. Yawns.*) Makes me feel so lazy ... Got a cigarette?

Abercrombie *takes a cigarette packet from trousers-pocket.*

Stella Give you one back ... Left em in me knickers.

Abercrombie *lights her cigarette with a lighter.*

Stella Foley not around? (*Blows out smoke.*)

Abercrombie Doubt it.

Stella Been in his office have you?

Abercrombie Not very often.

Stella Seen his jars. . . ? *Bottles* . . . Along the shelves . . .
Use them in chemistry labs, for acid.

Abercrombie Now you mention it.

Stella Full of urine.

Abercrombie What?

Stella Broke one, one day . . . cleaners. Terrible pong . . .
His lavatory . . . would you believe, is full of broken statues
. . . Venus de Milo in plaster-cast . . . all sorts of rubbish
he's collected.

Abercrombie Good God.

Stella Keeps his pee in bottles: anything artistic – down
the lav.

Abercrombie Good Lord.

Stella Suppose that's genius, really.

Abercrombie Yes . . .

Stella Modern art.

Pause.

Abercrombie That's right. (*Looks around for* **Allott**.)

Stella He was here not long ago . . . Mr Allott . . . Heard
him singing.

Abercrombie Singing?

Stella He sings, you know, when he's on his own . . .
Didn't know I was here, you see.

Abercrombie Ah, yes.

Stella What you use? (*Indicates racquet.*)

Abercrombie A rubber ball.

Stella   I've always been interested, you know, in sport . . .

Abercrombie   Ah, yes . . .

Stella   My own colour, that. (*Reveals her shoulder.*)

Abercrombie   Good lord.

Stella   I've a greasy skin. Just feel at that.

Abercrombie   It's very soft.

Stella   A woman should be soft.

Abercrombie   You've got very nice legs, of course.

Stella   They're not so bad . . . woman of my age. (*Shows him.*)

Abercrombie   Don't know why you bother with that. (*Indicates dressing-gown.*)

Stella   Can't sleep in me altogether. Not safe to in a place like this.

Abercrombie   One or two custodians of morality about.

Stella   Like who?

Abercrombie   Me.

Stella   Not from some of the tales I've heard.

Abercrombie   Such as?

Stella   Mr Abercrombie is a well-known character in some quarters of the town.

Abercrombie   The tennis courts are the only place I frequent with any regularity . . . and the squash courts, too, of course.

Stella *turns back to the screen.*

Abercrombie   Room for two in there?

Stella   There might.

Abercrombie   Have a smoke, I think, myself . . . Give it up . . . (*Coughs.*) Chest . . . Never persist for very long.

Stella   Sit, mind you. And nothing else.

Abercrombie *has gone behind the screen.*

Stella *follows.*

After a moment **Allott** *enters: slow. Takes hat off: sits down on edge of throne in his coat.*

Stella (*heard*)   Never . . . (*Laughter.*)

Abercrombie (*heard*)   As God is my witness.

Stella (*heard*)   All over?

Abercrombie (*heard*)   That's what the genius said. (*Laughter, heard.*)

Allott *glances up: no interest: sits with arms on his knees.* **Foley** *enters: stands there a moment, smoking pipe: takes it out.*

Foley   Bloody place is like a mausoleum.

Allott   Yes.

Foley   Lunch hour.

Allott   Yes.

Foley   Chisel-marks on that wall out theer . . . Bring them up, you know, from the sculpture room: safe-keeping in their lockers. What they do? Start taking the bloody place apart. (*Gazes round: finally looks up. Reads:*)

   'Foley is never sure
   Going to keep us solely
   On potato crisps for long.'

Chalk.

Allott   Yes.

Foley   Up yonder . . .

Allott (*looks*)   Yes.

Foley   Know the author?

Allott   No. (*Shakes his head.*)

Pause. **Foley** *looks round again. Pause.*

Foley   Disillusioning place, is this.

Allott   In what way?

Foley   Students of today ... two minutes with a bucket of plaster ... half a pot o' paint ... a bit o' wire ... turn out some conundrum on a piece of hardboard and think they've done a Mona Lisa. When you think this is where the Donatellos and the Verrocchios of the future are supposed to come from it begins to shake your faith.

Sits down on the throne beside **Allott**.

Ever think about life, then, do you?

Allott   (*hesitates for some considerable time. Then*)   No.

Foley   In my youth you thought of nothing else: life ... (*Gazes up. Pause.*) Infinity ... (*Pause. Abstracted. Then:*) Altered the pose, then, have you?

Allott   I thought I'd bear it in mind ... for a future occasion.

Foley   Classical, Allott. Classical. Every time. The distillation of history. The classical is the finest embodiment of the human spirit. That's what we're here to instil. A respect for the past and a clean and wholesome acceptance of the present ... Vegetarian?

Allott   (*looks up*)   No.

Foley   Do you know what's involved in the killing of a cow?

Allott   (*hesitates. Then*)   No.

Foley   The dismemberment of a living body?

Allott   No. (*Shakes his head.*)

Foley   I went to a butchery on one occasion ... I don't call it by any of these fancy names ... I went, ostensibly, to do some sketches – that's what I told the management – once there I found I couldn't draw a thing ... Blood there was. Everywhere ... intestines, bladders, stomachs, livers ... the appalling desecration of life ... the living reduced to an inanimate mass. (*Pause.*) Speak?

Allott No. (*Shakes his head.*)

Foley I've never touched a piece of meat since then. Every time a piece of meat is presented to me at table ... (*Takes out penknife.*) Cut my thumb.

Allott (*pause. Then*) Isn't it very dangerous?

Foley I disinfect the blade ... (*Shows him blade.*) Turns one or two stomachs, I can tell you that ... I use it occasionally, too, for sharpening pencils. (*Snaps blade to.*) Not in the dining-room, I thought, today.

Allott No.

Foley A consequence of illogical eating is illogical art. All good art is based on a good digestion. It's what these let-it-happen boys have never understood. Here today and gone tomorrow. They think abstraction, you know, can take art across national frontiers. Fact of the matter is, all the profoundest art is regional. It takes time for its universal principles to be revealed. For instance, who would have thought that a meticulous and obsessive interest in the Auvergne countryside would have made Cézanne one of the greatest – if not the greatest – painter of the present age. Draw a few rings, a few lines ... blocks of colour, and because it's immediately recognisable in Tokyo, Lisbon and New York, think it must be significant ... instant communication is the fallacy of the time. All these marvellous means for one human being to communicate with another – wireless, television, planes. What happens? Some terrible song-and-dance routine ... beyond that: aeons of triviality perpetuating itself across the vast distances of interstellar space.

Allott I didn't eat because my wife has decided to divorce me, as a matter of fact.

Foley Marriage for an artist is an anomaly in any case.

When a man's life is illuminated by an inner vision, everything outside is pure distraction.

Allott That's her opinion exactly . . . (*Gets up.*) She thinks – with my working here – I'm neither one thing nor another . . . My creations – including, I would have thought, my marriage – invisible events which only I can see . . .

Foley (*rising*) There's someone, you know, behind that screen. (*Goes over.*) Just look at this.

Stella (*heard*) Hello, Mr Foley.

Foley Not been smoking by any chance, then, have you?

Abercrombie (*heard*) No, sir. (*Comes out stretching, glancing at* **Allott**.) Fancy a shot or two, old man? (*Racquet.*)

Allott No, thanks.

Foley Smell smoke, you know, a mile off. I've an extremely sensitive nose for smoke. If somebody lights up a cigarette a mile off I can smell it in a matter of seconds.

Allott (*gazing up, reading*)
'Some talk of Alexander and some of Hercules,
But what of old Verrocchio and ancient Pericles?'

Foley *looks up too, and* **Abercrombie**.

Foley How they get up there beats me . . . It takes somebody more sophisticated than a student to think up rhymes like that.

Allott (*reading*)
'Teachers love to make a bit:
All students do is shovel . . .'

Foley It's not your casual two-minute composition that . . . there's fifteen-minutes' worth of lettering on that wall.

Allott (*reads, in a fresh direction*)
'Allott is a parrot,
Foley is a scream:
Abercrombie's like a carrot,

And Philips's just a queen.'

Foley Get the whitewash in here this evening. You can't turn your back on that. The Director of Education came in the other day. Know what was inscribed in the front doorway? 'Education is the opium of the middle classes.' My father was a cobbler, and, before that, his father was a blacksmith.

Abercrombie You've come a long way, Mr Foley.

Foley I have ... I have ... I'll not have them forget it ... (*Sees* **Abercrombie** *as if for the first time.*) You here for the Monte Carlo Rally, are you?

Abercrombie Squash.

Foley There's no squash in this building, I can tell you that. Sport and art don't mix. What stimulates the brain stimulates the body: you don't need to go chasing balls to keep fit ... We'll have that removed before I go tonight. (*Going: to* **Allott**.) Classical. Classical ... It's the eternal, Allott, that really lasts. (*Goes.*)

Allott *sits down. He's still got on his coat. Pause.*

Abercrombie *regards him for a moment. Then:*

Stella I think I'll go for a pee. (*Goes.*)

Abercrombie True?

Allott *looks up.*

Abercrombie Missis.

Allott My life has been a continual saga of good intentions, Abercrombie ... I only became an artist because I thought that way I'd be of least trouble to anybody else ... who's ever heard of an artist who's a liability?

Abercrombie Fancy a game or two, old man?

Allott Recline here, I think ... Swot up on one or two classical poses ... 'The Suicide's Revenge' ... 'Love in

Clover' . . . 'The Disinterested Man's Delight'.

Abercrombie Changeable situation . . . Might be back in time for bed.

Allott Not mine, I'm afraid. I'm sure of that.

Abercrombie Sure about the. . . ? (*Swings racquet.*)

Allott *nods.*

Abercrombie See you.

Allott See you.

Abercrombie *goes.*

Allott, *after a while, gets up: walks slowly round the stools. Finally sits down at one: gazes at the throne.*

Pause.

After a little while **Mathews** *comes in, whistling.*

Mathews Sir. (*Nods.*)

Allott *nods.*

Mathews Mind? (*Indicates donkey.*)

Allott Not really.

Mathews Stella. . . ? (*Nods at screen.*)

Allott *shakes his head.*

Mathews Fancy a bit of that . . . You know . . . time to time. Not above it when you catch her on her own. Other people around: screams blue murder. (*Pause.*) Seen Foley . . .

Allott Yes.

Mathews Tell you yesterday what happened?

Allott No . . .

Mathews Came in . . . late . . . School as quiet as death . . . tip-toe up the stairs: look behind . . . *entering* the hall below is a very large piece of . . . can you guess?

Allott, *after some moments' hesitation, shakes his head.*

Mathews Coal . . . (*Waits for* **Allott**'s *reaction.*) Two hands clasped to this gigantic piece of coal . . . big as a house . . . Know who it was? . . . Foley! . . . head comes in view . . . Looks this way . . . looks that . . . coal held out . . . looks up. Sees me. Know what he does? . . . Steps *backwards* . . . Couldn't believe it. Ever so slowly. After a few seconds this gigantic lump of coal just disappears . . . I go on up the stairs . . . Mark time. Steps get fainter . . . Two minutes later . . . piece of coal comes back . . . two hands . . . Foley . . . Tuck my head in . . . Steps out across the hall . . . Let him get half way . . . Call: '*Mr Foley, have you got a minute?*' . . . Should have seen it . . . crash like thunder . . . Look down . . . bits of coal all over the hall . . . Next thing: belting up the stairs and calling: '*Anybody smoking up here, then, is there?*' (*Laughs.*)

Allott *no reaction.*

Pause.

Mathews Tell me he's a kleptomaniac.

Allott Is that so?

Mathews Catch him one day.

Allott Sure to.

Mathews Be in for the high-jump: can tell you that.

Allott There are plans, as a matter of fact, to replace this college with an Institute of Engineering . . . the designs are quite advanced, I understand . . . octagonal building with vertical lighting – no windows except in the roof – and a large gallery at one end for the mounting of exceptionally large pieces of machinery . . . what we want, in a nutshell, but it'll be given over exclusively to engines.

Mathews *has mounted the throne.*

Mathews Fancied modelling, you know, myself . . . Do muscle exercises in the evening . . . (*Poses.*) . . . no threat of redundancy . . . alus somebody to look at somebody else.

Allott Yes.

Pause. He gazes at **Mathews**.

If you stand there for a moment . . . (*Takes out pad, pencil.*)

Mathews (*poses*) This do you?

Allott Anything that comes natural.

Mathews *poses.*

Allott *draws casually. Silence.*

Mathews Strip down if you like.

Allott I think this'll do perfectly . . . you're posing very well.

Mathews Think I'm loud-mouthed . . . (*Gestures off.*) Them . . . Fact is – do you mind me talking? – you act up to what people expect of you.

Allott How do you know what they expect?

Mathews Feel it . . .

Allott Suppose you're mistaken?

Mathews Not here.

Allott Suppose really they'd been expecting someone different?

Mathews How different?

Allott Sensitive . . . intelligent . . . (*Still drawing.*) perhaps even quietly mannered.

Mathews My looks?

Allott Looks can be deceptive.

Mathews Long-distance only . . .

Allott Seen that wall?

Mathews One o' your rhymes.

Allott Hardly.

Mathews What?

Allott Not that tall.

Mathews (*reads*) 'O where has the significance of life gone to . . .'

Allott (*without looking up*) 'My mother said.'

Mathews '. . . If it's not where we might expect it, it must be in some other place instead.'

Allott Moving.

Mathews Oh . . . Yeh. (*Adjusts his pose.*)

Allott That's better . . . No. No. That's fine. (*Draws in silence for a while.*)

Philips *comes in.*

Philips Bet on . . . Odds as mentioned . . . (*Sees* **Mathews**.) Carter.

Mathews Mathews.

Philips Mathews. (*Gazes at* **Mathews** *for some time.*)

Mathews (*finally, under* **Philips**' *gaze*) Mind if I get down, sir?

Allott One more minute.

Mathews Arms ache.

Allott Ten seconds.

Mathews Harder than you think.

Philips When I was in the pink could stand, utterly immobile, for an hour and a half . . . Reflex: a conditioned reflex. What's required, ironically enough, is to be utterly relaxed.

Allott Five.

Philips I've got the slip . . . Lucky Horseshoe . . .

Allott I'll never need it.

Philips   Odds had shortened before I left. Sevens. It'll be three to one by the time they reach the post.

Allott   Two.

Mathews   I'm going dizzy.

Allott   Hold it. Hold it.

Mathews, *after a strenuous effort to keep still, collapses.*

Allott *goes on drawing for a moment.*

Mathews *sits moaning, massaging.*

Allott *finally looks up: looks about him. Then:*

Allott   Take this off . . . (*Coat: stands: removes it.*) Hang it. (*Feels in his pockets.*) Shan't be long. (*Goes.*)

Mathews   First time I've seen his drawing.

Philips   One of the leading exponents of representational art in his youth, was Mr Allott . . . You'd have to go back to Michelangelo to find a suitable comparison . . .

Mathews *stoops over pad: peers closely.*

Mathews   There's nothing there . . .

Philips   Now, of course . . . an impresario . . . purveyor of the invisible event . . . so far ahead of his time you never see it.

Mathews   I've been posing there for half an hour!

Philips   Longer, I'd imagine.

Mathews (*picks up pad: examines other pages. Reads finally*)
'Oh, she was good all right in patches,
She was good all right in bed:
But where would it all have ended
If I'd loved her like I said?'

Philips   I really think that's private property, old boy.

Mathews (*reads*)
'Oh, we'll listen to the wireless

And lie in bed till three;
"Turn up the volume, lady."
Oh, love is good to me.'

Evades **Philips**' *effort to take the pad.*

'Oh, he found love in valleys,
In caves and crannies too;
Fissures, where a lover
Could find what lovers do.'

Philips I think, really, that belongs to me ... is in my custody ... my supervision.

Mathews (*reads*)
'He called her night and morning;
He sat beside the phone:
What's mine is yours, she told him:
Oh, give a dog a bone!'

Philips I'm appealing to you, Mathews, as a member of the staff ... as a respected and somewhat elderly member of the staff ... lightweight champion of the northern counties and – for several months previous to that – of one of the more prominent of the southern counties as well.

Mathews (*reads*)
'He waited, how he waited;
He waited for his love:
She'd meant to get there early,
But went back for her glove.'

Philips See here, Mathews ... That's private property.

Mathews Here ... just look at this. (*Shows it to* **Philips**.)

Philips (*reads*) 'I shall kill Foley ... Foley is very poorly ... Foley is surely ... the person I shall hourly ... kill ... whenever poor old Allott gets the chance ...'

Mathews 'Poor old Allott is the ...'

Philips 'Apotheosis ...'

Mathews 'Poor old Allott is the ...'

Philips 'Amanuensis . . .'

Mathews 'Poor old Allott is the . . .'

Philips 'Polarity . . .'

Mathews 'From which this world began . . .'

Philips 'Poor old Al . . .'

Mathews 'Poor old Allott . . .'

Philips 'Dirge on a forgotten planet . . .'

Mathews 'Allott is the palette . . .'

Philips 'On which my sins began . . .'

Mathews 'First . . .'

Philips 'He was a saviour . . .'

Mathews 'Secondly . . .'

Philips 'A saint . . .'

Mathews 'Thirdly . . .'

Philips 'Lost his chances . . .'

Mathews 'Fourthly . . .'

Philips 'Learnt to paint.'

Mathews 'Fifthly . . .'

Philips 'Came to pieces . . .'

Mathews 'Sixthly . . .'

Philips 'Showed his hand.'

Mathews 'Seventhly . . .'

Philips 'Set his creases . . .'

Mathews 'Eighthly . . .'

Philips 'Joined the band.'

Mathews 'Ninthly . . .'

Philips 'Went to heaven . . .'

Mathews 'Tenthly . . .'

Philips 'Rang the bell.'

Mathews 'Eleventhly . . .'

Philips 'Thought he'd better . . .'

Mathews 'Twelfthly . . .'

Allott (*having entered*) 'Go to hell' . . . No, no, really, Philips . . . Once started, carry on . . .

Philips I was trying to get it from him. I was even – would you believe it – threatening him with physical violence.

Mathews Private, sir. (*Hands it back.*) I was just looking at the drawing, sir.

Allott There isn't any drawing . . . or, rather, the drawing was the drawing . . . perhaps you weren't aware.

Mathews No, sir. (*Pause. Then:*) I'll go and get my board, sir.

Allott Right.

Mathews *hesitates: glances from one to the other: goes.*

Philips (*examines watch*) Better be getting back . . . Proceedings start in seven minutes . . . Six and a half to be exact . . . Carter moved the platform slightly.

Allott Mathews.

Philips Mathews . . . (*Adjusts it slightly.*) Right . . . (*Glances round.*) See you.

Allott See you.

Philips *looks round once more: nods: goes.*

Allott *stays precisely where he is, standing.*

Long pause.

In the silence, eventually, **Stella** *comes in.*

Stella   No one here?

Allott   We're ready.

Stella   Want me up?

Allott   Pose.

Stella *climbs on to the throne: disrobes. Stands there. Then:*

Stella   How do you want me?

Allott   Natural.

Stella *poses.*

Stella   Where are the others?

Allott   Coming.

Saunders *enters. Moves round self-consciously in duffle-coat, board beneath his arm: considers which of the donkeys he might take.*

Saunders   Snowing.

Allott   Really?

Saunders   Outside ... Stella.

Stella   Hello, Samuel.

Saunders   The name's Terry. Samuel or Sammy is a nickname given me by the students.

Stella   I'm sorry, Terry.

Saunders   Do you mind if I sit here?

Stella   Keep an eye on you.

Saunders   I prefer to see your face ... I don't like human beings to be set down as objects ... Are you drawing as well, Mr Allott?

Allott   I ... create, Saunders, in an altogether different dimension.

Saunders *settles himself. Pause. Then:*

Saunders The human condition ... is made up of many ambivalent conditions ... that's one thing I've discovered ... love, hatred ... despair, hope ... exhilaration, anguish ... and it's not these conditions themselves that are of any significance but the fact that, as human beings, we oscillate between them ... It's the oscillation between hope and despair that's the great feature of our existence, not the hope, or the despair, in themselves.

Pause.

Stella It's a wonderful observation ...

Pause. **Saunders** *settles himself: gets out his equipment.*

I like people who think about life.

Saunders I don't think about life. I'm merely interested in recording it.

Stella I see.

Saunders *sets up his plumb-line and strings, etc., facing* **Stella**.

Saunders I think Mr Allott is quite correct: all great art is truly impersonal. All great *lives* are impersonal ... To live truly you have to be ...

Allott Impersonal.

Saunders It's only the disinterested person who sees what's truly there. I learnt that from you, sir.

Allott Yes.

Saunders These others have no regard for anything ... They have no *conception* of those qualities which can lift a man above his habitual animal existence.

Allott No.

Saunders Can you lift your head a bit higher, Stella ...

Stella Like this?

Saunders (*examines her for a while in silence. Then*) Yes.

Roar outside: **Mathews**, **Warren**, **Mooney**, **Gillian**,

Brenda and **Catherine** enter in a noisy group. **Warren**: 'All over the bloody floor!' *Laughter.*

Gillian   We've started.

Allott   To your donkeys, men . . .

Mathews blows raspberry. Laughter.

Catherine   Sir! It's a new one.

Brenda   The light's all different.

Allott   Sufficient unto the day is the evil thereof, Catherine.

Catherine   Sir! I've got to start all over again. . . !

Warren   Improvise.

Allott   Improvisation is the hallmark of the bereft imagination . . . Draw, Catherine . . . Brenda . . . Warren . . . Carter . . . Mathews . . . Mooney . . . Gillian . . . Draw. Register, merely, what you see before you.

Mathews blows raspberry: laughter.

Warren (calling)   How are you, Sammy?

Saunders   All right.

Brenda   Brought your binoculars, have you?

Mathews   Now, then. Now, then. What have we got here? (*Rubs hands, gazes at* **Stella**, *standing over his donkey.*) Head, hands, feet, two tits . . . a pair o' smashers . . . all correct and ready to go. (*Salutes: raspberry: gets down to it.*)

Silence slowly descends: **Warren** *belches: laughter.*

Silence descends again. Then:

Brenda   Quiet, i'n it?

Laughter. Silence grows again: snigger – muffled; titter – muffled.

Long pause.

Whatch'a have, then?

Gillian Sago.

Warren Terrible.

Mathews Never eat here.

Carter Go to the Excelsior myself.

Catherine That restaurant?

Carter Snack-bar ... soup, coffee: that's all you need for lunch.

Warren (*belches*) To the pub, personally, myself.

Mooney Can't afford it.

Mathews Catering for two.

Mooney Piss off.

Warren *belches.*

They go on drawing.

Allott *stands at the back: abstracted.*

Silence.

Gillian You've got a spot, Stella.

Stella Where?

Gillian Left leg.

Carter Look at it *later.*

Catherine Inside your knee.

Stella Oh ... yes!

Brenda I've got some ointment.

Carter Later.

Warren Later!

Catherine Honestly!

Stella *gazes at them: resumes her pose.*

Silence. Then:

Mathews   What you drawing, Gillian?

Gillian   Not you.

Mooney   Leave her alone, fart-face.

Mathews (*to* **Mooney**: *makes a fist*)   Push this up your nose.

Mooney   Push it up somewhere else might be more useful.

Mathews   Look! (*Rises threateningly.*)

Allott (*stepping forward*)   I thought – with your permission – I might pose myself.

Catherine   Sir!

Brenda   Sir.

Catherine   How super!

Gillian   Not in the nude, sir!

Allott   Why not?

Catherine   Oh . . . sir!

Warren   Go on, sir . . . Let 'em have it!

Allott   I thought it might be an inducement . . .

Brenda   Sir!

Allott   The sort, Brenda, of whose absence you were complaining only a little while ago.

Catherine   Sir! You can't.

Mathews   Here . . . go on, sir. I'll come up with you!

Mathews *springs up on to the throne:*

Screams: roars of laughter.

Stella *descends, screaming: snatches her dressing-gown.*

The girls laugh: **Warren** *shouts encouragement:* 'Go on!'

Mathews   Five-minute poses. Who's gonna keep the

time?

Brenda   Stop him, sir. Stop him.

Mathews *has begun to remove his clothes.*

Warren   Get it out then, Matty! Get it out!

Mathews   Who'll join me, then! Who'll join me!

Laughter: jeers.

Saunders   It's the dividing line, you see, between life and art ... Stella represents it in its impersonal condition ... Mathews represents its ...

Warren   Get your prick out ...! Here ... here, then. Go on. Grab her.

Has already risen: seizes **Stella** *and forces her back, struggling, to the throne.*

Laughter.

Mathews   Here, come on, let's have a hold as well!

They struggle with the screaming **Stella** *between them.*

Catherine   Sir ...! Stop him, sir!

Warren   Go on, then ... Get it out, then, Mathews ... get it in.

Mathews   I can't ... I can't ...

Laughter.

Warren   Lie still, for God's sake ...

Stella   Get off ... (*Screaming.*) Get off!

Warren   Get it in, for God's sake.

Mathews   I am. I am.

Stella   Get off ... Get off ... Get him off.

Warren   Go on: thump it. Thump it.

Mathews   I am! ... I am! (*Still struggling to straddle* **Stella**.)

Stella *laughs, half-screams at* **Mathews'** *efforts.*

Allott *stands, pausing, halfway between the donkeys and the throne.*

Saunders *gazes transfixed.*

Carter *calls out encouragement, laughing.*

Gillian *gazes, blank, uncomprehending.*

Mooney *has stepped forward as if he might intervene.*

Brenda's *got up: crossed halfway and stays there.*

Catherine *stays sitting, her pen still in her hand.*

Warren   Get it in ... Get it in ... thump it, Mathews ... thump it ...

Mathews   Hold her! Hold her!

Stella   Get off ... Get him off.

Warren   Get your legs open, Stella.

Stella   Get him off.

Warren   Get it in, for God's sake.

Stella   No ... No ...

Mathews   I am! ... I am! ... Oh God ... Here! ... It's lovely.

Catherine   Sir! Sir!

Warren   Thump it!

Mathews   *I am! I am!*

Brenda   Sir ... For God's sake, sir ...

Catherine   Fetch Mr Foley!

Warren   Thump it! Thump it ... Go on, Matt ... Here. Come on ... let's have a go!

Gillian   Sir! Tell him to stop it. Sir! ... Tell him!

Warren   Here ... here ... Come on. Let's have it!

Mathews I'm coming ... I'm coming! ... God ... Oh God ... I'm coming...! Hold her ... Hold her.

Stella No ... *No!*

Catherine Sir! Sir! For God's sake, sir!

Mathews Oh! (*Falls, moaning, over her. Moans: his movements slow. Slows: stillness.*)

Warren Jesus ... Look ... He has, an' all ... Bloody hell. Didn't think he had it in him. Cor blimey, Mathews ... (*Laughs.*)

Catherine *sits dumbfounded.*

Gillian *has covered her face with her hands.*

Mooney Jesus ... (*Turns to* **Carter**.)

Carter *The dirty bugger.*

Mooney *The dirty sod.*

Saunders *still sits there, dazed.*

Carter *hasn't moved.*

Warren *stands by the throne, contemplating* **Mathews**, *seemingly incredulous: stoops over* **Stella** *finally.*

Warren You all right, Stell?

Brenda *still sits there, gazing at* **Stella**.

Mathews, *bowed, raises his head: gazes at the others: smiles; then, straightening, he breaks into laughter.*

Warren *breaks into laughter: dances down from platform.*

Warren Had you! Had you...! Thought he had...! (*Dances in front of* **Brenda**, **Catherine**.)

Mathews *sits, cross-legged on the platform, laughing.*

Warren Thought he'd had her, didn't you, love!

Brenda You dirty filthy beast. Disgusting ... (*To* **Allott**.) It's disgusting, sir.

Warren   She thought you'd had it in there, Mathews. (*To* **Brenda**.) Give us something to go home with, love.

Catherine   How could you! Let him do it, sir!

Warren   Had her going. Didn't we, love!

Brenda   Piss off.

Mathews   Stick of dynamite. (*Flourishes himself: fanfare.*)

Warren *and* **Mathews** *laugh.*

Allott   If you wouldn't mind ... Stella ... (*Invites her to resume her pose.*)

Warren (*to* **Stella**)   Lit her fuse then, have we, love?

Stella   Get off!

Gillian   I think it was obscene, vulgar and disgusting.

Warren   It's the on'y three words she bloody knows.

Catherine   Why did you let him do it, sir? Why did you start him off?

Allott *gazes at them.*

Mathews *has climbed down from the throne, straightening his clothes, laughing.*

Allott   My own effort was to have been altogether less sensational ... That's to say, dispassionate ... (*Quieter.*) ... I would have posed for you quite gladly ... as it is ...

Catherine   Here ... are you all right, sir?

Allott   The essence of any event, Catherine ... is that it should be ... indefinable. Such is the nature ... the ambivalence – as Saunders so aptly described it – of all human responses ... love, hate ... anguish ... hope? Was it hope you made a corollary of anguish...? Far be it from me to intrude ... my domestic circumstance ... my personal life is my own affair ... can play no part in what, to all intents and purposes, may well be happening here ... a personal element which, despite all my efforts, I

cannot ... understandably ... restrain ... thorn within the
flesh ... The prospect of presenting myself to you, even
now, in what may be described as a human condition isn't
all that repellent to me ... It's merely that ... it would no
longer be, as it were, a work of art ... merely ... another
aspect of a human being. (*Pause. Then:*) I suppose the best
solution ... Warren ... Mathews ... is to return to the
job in hand ... I to instruct; you to be instructed ...
Stella.

Stella *looks round.*

Mathews *and* **Warren** *have returned to their donkeys: silence.*

Allott *straightens the throne: positions and straightens the white cloth:
pauses: waits.*

Stella, *after a moment's hesitation, climbs up: glances at the
students: disrobes: takes up her pose.*

Then, in the silence:

Saunders   Head to the left, Stella ... Arm ...

Stella *follows* **Saunders**' *instructions.*

Saunders   That's right.

Allott   If you'd resume your various ... and singularly
varied ...

Pause.

They begin to draw.

No work of art is complete without a personal statement.
After all, the tradition we're ostensibly working in here is
one which declares art to be a residual occupation ... that
is to say, it leaves objects – certain elements of its activity –
behind ... stone, paint, canvas ... bronze ... paper ...
carbon ... a synthesis of natural elements convened by
man ... whereas we, elements as it were of a work
ourselves, partake of existence ... simply by being what we
are ... expressions of a certain time and place, and class
... defying ... hope ... defying anguish ... defying, even,

definition . . . more substantial than reality . . . stranger
than a dream . . . figures in a landscape . . . scratching . . .
scraping . . . rubbing . . . All around us . . . our rocky ball
. . . hurtling through time . . . Singing . . . to no one's tune
at all.

Fade.

Dark.

Scene Two

*Light comes up: as before: throne, donkeys, heaters, easels, screens:
empty. After a while* **Brenda** *comes in: coat on, canvas bag.*

Brenda   Gone.

Catherine *enters: coat, cap, bag.*

Catherine   No use waiting.

Brenda   Hang on.

She goes to upstage screen:

Saunders *enters: coat on, scarf.*

Saunders   Hey: what're you doing?

Brenda   Piss off.

Brenda *brings out* **Stella***'s bags from behind the screen.*

Catherine   Has Mr Allott gone?

Saunders   He's in Foley's office.

Brenda   You report it, Sammy? (*Hands one of the bags to*
Catherine.)

Saunders   Somebody's got to be responsible for decency
and order.

Catherine   Lose his job, I shouldn't wonder.

Brenda   Pity somebody, Saunders, didn't lose something
else.

Saunders   Allott's trouble is that he's got no discipline. He lets his theories run away with him. Art and life, in that respect, are separate things. No one should allow life to monopolise art: and similarly no one should allow art to be engulfed by life.

Brenda   You in charge in here?

Saunders *has begun to straighten the donkeys: takes white sheet from the throne: begins to fold it.*

Saunders   It would have been reported in any case. I'm not averse to taking on that responsibility. Somebody has to do it. Even if it puts them in bad odour with everybody else . . . They'll need this place, in any case, tomorrow.

Catherine   What for?

Brenda   Another orgy.

Saunders   To create something out of chaos, Catherine . . . To invigorate. Distil. Not to deprave. To illuminate. Art, Catherine, should be an example. Not a reflection. If life itself is degenerate then art should set ideals.

Brenda   He *is* taking over. (*To* **Catherine**.) Got your hat?

Allott *enters: coat over arm, hat and gloves in hand.*

Pause.

They wait: **Saunders** *goes on tidying up.*

Allott   What are you doing with that?

Catherine   They're Stella's, sir.

Allott   She's quite capable of collecting them herself.

Brenda   She didn't want to come up, sir.

Allott   She's got two arms, two legs; there's nothing to prevent her.

Catherine   We thought it'd be kinder to take them down.

Allott I think, on the whole, it might be kinder to leave them here.

They hesitate: glance at each other: put the bags down.

Brenda We came up to say good night, sir.

Allott Good night.

Pause: **Catherine** *and* **Brenda** *look at one another. Then:*

Catherine Good night, then, sir.

They go.

Saunders *works, tidying.*

Allott *watches a moment. Then:*

Allott I have to thank you, evidently . . . for taking the part of public decency and order in this matter. Saunders.

Saunders That's right.

Allott I thought, on the whole, you enjoyed it. Gave you something to speculate about . . . All the artist needs, after all, is *meat* — something to react to, report on, comment about, differentiate between . . . *record* . . . he never has to act. At least, that's how I've always understood it.

Saunders Perhaps we're talking, sir, about a different kind of art.

Allott Evidently. I've lost my job.

Saunders I'm sorry to hear that, sir.

Allott So am I. I've lost a wife . . . I've also lost my sole means, if it were at all desirable, of supporting her. It seems I'll have to dig deeper into my already somewhat limited resources and find what other potentialities might be lying there . . . as a revolutionary and a leader of the avant-garde — purveyor of the invisible event, marching ahead of my time — it seems my already overtaxed imagination has not been taxed enough.

Saunders (*looking round*) If there's nothing else, I'll go.

Allott   That's very kind.

The room is tidy: pause.

Saunders   Good night, then, sir.

Allott   Good night.

Saunders *goes to the exit. Then:*

Saunders   If you should ever feel the need to discuss why I acted like I did I'll always be available, sir.

Allott   You better go, Saunders . . . Your kindness . . . positively . . . overwhelms me. Any further display of it will reduce me – I can assure you, Saunders – to something very little short of tears.

Saunders   Good night, then, sir. (*Goes.*)

Allott *stands there a moment: stiff, expectant.* **Carter** *enters.*

Carter   I'm off, sir.

Allott (*looks up*)   Right.

Carter   Sorry to hear about your difference with the Principal, sir.

Allott   Scarcely a difference, Carter.

Carter   No, sir.

Allott   More in the nature I would have thought of a final solution.

Carter   Anything I can do, sir?

Allott (*looks round: donkeys in a neat row: throne straight, sheet folded*)   It seems everything's been done.

Carter (*hesitates. Then*)   Good night, then, sir.

Allott   Good night, Carter.

Carter *nods, hesitates, then goes: laughter, whistling, cries, jeers off.*

Warren *enters, followed a moment later by* **Mathews**: *evidently they've been tussling with* **Carter**, *off.*

Warren Night, sir!

Allott Night, Warren.

Mathews Just popped in, sir. Say cheerio.

Allott Cheerio.

Warren Sorry to hear the news, sir.

Allott That's right.

Mathews Any time you want a reference, sir.

Allott I'll not forget.

Warren You're the tops for us, sir.

Mathews Every time!

Laughter: horse with each other.

Warren Night, sir.

Mathews Night, sir.

Allott Good night.

They go: pass **Philips** *entering:* 'Night, Mr Philips!' 'Night, Mr Philips, sir!' *Laughter.*

Philips *is wrapped up: coat, cap, scarf.*

Philips Sevens, old boy! (*Thumbs up.*)

Allott Snow, of course, could easily postpone it.

Philips Snow, old boy: hadn't thought of that ... Still. (*Claps gloved hands.*) Ours not to reason.

Allott No, old man.

Philips Well ... See you, Allott.

Allott See you.

Philips (*hesitates. Then*) Good night. (*Goes.*)

Allott *looks round: one last donkey marginally out of line: carefully adjusts it: lines it up exactly: squints along it: adjusts it once again. Readjusts.*

Then: **Abercrombie** *enters: wrapped up, no bowler hat.*

Abercrombie   Seen Foley?

Allott   Some rearrangement of the curriculum, it appears, is being considered ... as the result 'of certain unedifying scenes observed by at least one member of the student body ... as a consequence of which a somewhat more traditional form of life-class may well be introduced ... Revolution, after all, is not a self-perpetuating process ... it does, by definition, they tell me, come to an end.

Abercrombie   That's right.

Allott   I've always seen myself as something of a pilgrim ... a goal so mystical it defies description ... not gates, exactly, I see before me ... more nearly, Abercrombie ... (*Gazes directly at him.*) a pair of eyes. (*Pause. Examines* **Abercrombie**. *Then:*) I attempted to negotiate ... true instinct of the employee ... scenes of rape ... masturbatory tendencies evident amongst my pupils which I made no attempt to discourage – if anything, according to reports, I did everything to stimulate ... bartering silence over *my* chef d'oeuvre if I gave to the authorities no information about our Principal's own cloacal masterpiece – toilet seat a pedestal for one of the more lyrical outpourings of Praxiteles ... Decency in the end, Abercrombie, you'll be pleased to hear, prevailed. Mr Foley is cleaning up his toilet – leaving no evidence, as it were, behind. No artist, after all, I decided, should condemn another ... We are all, I've come to realise, *brothers* ... even if some, it transpires, have to be more brotherly than others ... Michelangelo's *David* and Caravaggio's *Disciples at Emmaus* – to name but two – were not that easily come by: they were the process of a great deal of mental pain. I shall let that anguish, Abercrombie, go before me ... Go before me and – if the past is anything to go by – light my way.

Mooney *enters, followed by* **Gillian** *holding his hand.*

Mooney   I came to say good night, sir.

Allott   Good night, Mooney ... Good night, Gillian.

Mooney *waits for* **Gillian** *to answer.*

Gillian   All I wanted to say, sir.

Allott   Yes?

Gillian   I don't hold you to blame, sir.

Allott   That's very commendable.

Gillian   It's the circumstances, sir.

Allott   That's quite correct ... But then, in a way,
Gillian, I created them. That, after all, is my modus
operandi ... preparation ... assembly ... pound, grind,
mix ... colour sublimated somewhat by the immediate
surround ... partaking nevertheless – to some extent – of
our ... relatively, Gillian ... unadulterated nature ...
yours, and yours ... and ... (*Pauses: indicates*
Abercrombie.) his ... My next work may be something
altogether less commendable ... That's to say, more ...
substantial ... if not altogether more extravagant than what
I appear to have achieved today ... I shall have to see ...
sans means ... sans wife ... sans recognition who's to
know what I ... might rise to ...

Pause. Then:

Mooney   We wish you luck, sir.

Allott   Thank you, Mooney.

Gillian   Good night, then, sir.

Allott   Good night, Gillian.

They hesitate: glance at **Allott** *once more: nod, then go.*

Abercrombie   I suppose I better go as well ... Anything
I can do?

Allott   Ahead of its time ... impossible to perceive ...
the pageant is at an end now, Abercrombie ... The
process, as you can see, is virtually complete.

Abercrombie *gazes around him. Then:*

Abercrombie   See you, sport.

Allott   See you.

Abercrombie *nods, smiles, and goes.*

Allott *pauses: sits.*

Silence.

After a while **Stella** *enters: dressed for the cold: coat, scarf, gloves, beret. Nods at* **Allott**: *goes to screen.*

Allott   If you're looking for these, I've got them here.

Stella   Said they'd brought them down. Looked all over.

Allott   Recovered, have you?

Stella   Think so. (*Tucking her hair beneath her beret, ready to leave.*)

Allott   Violation, they tell me, is a prerequisite of art . . . disruption of prevailing values . . . re-integration in another form entirely. What you see and feel becomes eternal . . . a flower grows . . . a million million years it takes to blossom . . . (*Waits.*) Will you be coming up tomorrow?

Stella   I suppose so . . . (*Checks bags.*) Shopping . . . (*Examines contents.*) . . . (*Looks up.*) See you, Mr Allott.

Allott   See you.

(*As* **Stella** *goes.*) Would you . . . (*She pauses, turning.*) . . . put out the light?

Pauses: nods: she goes: a moment later the light diminishes.

Allott *stands: pulls on his coat: puts on his hat.*

Foley *enters in the half-light.*

Foley   Still here, are you.

Pause: he gazes round.

Allott   That's right.

Foley *gazes overhead for a while. Then:*

Foley   Thought of writing one up myself. (*Nods at wall.*) 'When is a man not a man?' (*Pause.*) I could never think of a second line.

Allott   That's right.

Foley   It's not without some regret . . . (*Gestures to him.*) You leaving.

Allott   No.

Foley   I hope you'll find your next appointment more rewarding.

Allott   I don't know . . . It's had its compensations, Principal . . . I've achieved some of my best work, I think, in here.

Foley   I believe in forgiveness, Allott . . . Apart from a good digestion, it's the one indispensable principle of human growth.

Allott   That's right.

Foley   A man – if he puts his mind to it – can always mend his ways. Experience, you see, can put you right . . . In here, the mind atrophies, hardens: when the soul is constipated it means the nourishment isn't right.

Allott   I'll keep my bowels open.

Foley   It'll make a difference, I can tell you that . . . You'll leave the life-room tidy? (*Waits for* **Allott**'s *acknowledgement.*) Set an example, otherwise no one follows. (*Puts out his hand.*) I better say good night.

Allott   Good night, Principal. (*Shakes his hand.*)

Foley *looks round, briskly: nods: he goes.*

Allott *looks round: draws on his gloves: pulls up his collar: looks round once again, freshly: goes.*

Fade.

Methuen Contemporary Dramatists
include

Peter Barnes (three volumes)
Sebastian Barry
Edward Bond (six volumes)
Howard Brenton
  (two volumes)
Richard Cameron
Jim Cartwright
Caryl Churchill (two volumes)
Sarah Daniels (two volumes)
David Edgar (three volumes)
Dario Fo (two volumes)
Michael Frayn (two volumes)
Peter Handke
Jonathan Harvey
Declan Hughes
Terry Johnson
Bernard-Marie Koltès
Doug Lucie
David Mamet (three volumes)

Anthony Minghella
  (two volumes)
Tom Murphy (four volumes)
Phyllis Nagy
Peter Nichols (two volumes)
Philip Osment
Louise Page
Stephen Poliakoff
  (three volumes)
Christina Reid
Philip Ridley
Willy Russell
Ntozake Shange
Sam Shepard (two volumes)
David Storey (three volumes)
Sue Townsend
Michel Vinaver (two volumes)
Michael Wilcox

Methuen World Classics
include

Jean Anouilh (two volumes)
John Arden (two volumes)
Arden & D'Arcy
Brendan Behan
Aphra Behn
Bertolt Brecht (six volumes)
Büchner
Bulgakov
Calderón
Anton Chekhov
Noël Coward (five volumes)
Eduardo De Filippo
Max Frisch
Gorky
Harley Granville Barker
   (two volumes)
Henrik Ibsen (six volumes)
Lorca (three volumes)
Marivaux

Mustapha Matura
David Mercer (two volumes)
Arthur Miller (five volumes)
Molière
Musset
Clifford Odets
Joe Orton
A. W. Pinero
Luigi Pirandello
Terence Rattigan
W. Somerset Maugham
   (two volumes)
Wole Soyinka
August Strindberg
   (three volumes)
J. M. Synge
Ramón del Valle-Inclán
Frank Wedekind
Oscar Wilde

METHUEN DRAMA
ANTON CHEKHOV

☐ CHEKHOV PLAYS (*The Seagull, Uncle Vanya, Three Sisters, The Cherry Orchard* and four vaudevilles)

Translated and introduced by Michael Frayn £7.99

☐ THE CHERRY ORCHARD   Methuen Student Edition

Translated and introduced by Michael Frayn £5.99

☐ THE CHERRY ORCHARD   Methuen Theatre Classics

Translated and introduced by Michael Frayn £5.99

☐ IVANOV   Methuen Modern Play

Adapted by David Hare £6.99

☐ DEAR WRITER, DEAR ACTRESS

The Love Letters of Anton Chekhov and Olga Knipper

Selected, edited and translated by Jean Benedetti £10.99

METHUEN CLASSICAL GREEK DRAMATISTS

☐ AESCHYLUS PLAYS: I (*Persians, Prometheus Bound, Suppliants, Seven Against Thebes*) £9.99
☐ AESCHYLUS PLAYS: II (*Oresteia: Agamemnon, Libation-Bearers, Eumenides*) £9.99
☐ SOPHOCLES PLAYS: I (*Oedipus the King, Oedipus at Colonus, Antigone*) £9.99
☐ SOPHOCLES PLAYS: II (*Ajax, Women of Trachis, Electra, Philoctetes*) £9.99
☐ EURIPIDES PLAYS: I (*Medea, The Phoenician Women, Bacchae*) £9.99
☐ EURIPIDES PLAYS: II (*Hecuba, The Women of Troy, Iphigenia at Aulis, Cyclops*) £9.99
☐ EURIPIDES PLAYS: III (*Alkestis, Helen, Ion*) £9.99
☐ EURIPIDES PLAYS: IV (*Elektra, Orestes, Iphigeneia in Tauris*) £9.99
☐ EURIPIDES PLAYS: V (*Andromache, Herakles' Children, Herakles*) £9.99
☐ EURIPIDES PLAYS: VI (*Hippolytos Suppliants, Rhesos*) £9.99
☐ ARISTOPHANES PLAYS: I (*Acharnians, Knights, Peace, Lysistrata*) £9.99
☐ ARISTOPHANES PLAYS: II (*Wasps, Clouds, Birds, Festival Time, Frogs*) £9.99
☐ ARISTOPHANES & MENANDER: NEW COMEDY
(Aristophanes: *Women in Power, Wealth*
Menander: *The Malcontent, The Woman from Samos*) £9.99

• All Methuen Drama books are available through mail order or from your local bookshop.

Please send cheque/eurocheque/postal order (sterling only) Access, Visa, Mastercard, Diners Card, Switch or Amex.

☐☐☐☐☐☐☐☐☐☐☐☐☐☐☐☐

Expiry Date: _____ Signature: _____

Please allow 75 pence per book for post and packing U.K.
Overseas customers please allow £1.00 per copy for post and packing.

ALL ORDERS TO:
Methuen Books, Books by Post, TBS Limited, The Book Service, Colchester Road, Frating Green, Colchester, Essex CO7 7DW.

NAME: _____

ADDRESS: _____

_____

_____

Please allow 28 days for delivery. Please tick box if you do not
wish to receive any additional information ☐

Prices and availability subject to change without notice.

METHUEN STUDENT EDITIONS

☐ SERJEANT MUSGRAVE'S DANCE	John Arden	£6.99
☐ CONFUSIONS	Alan Ayckbourn	£5.99
☐ THE ROVER	Aphra Behn	£5.99
☐ LEAR	Edward Bond	£6.99
☐ THE CAUCASIAN CHALK CIRCLE	Bertolt Brecht	£6.99
☐ MOTHER COURAGE AND HER		
CHILDREN	Bertolt Brecht	£6.99
☐ THE CHERRY ORCHARD	Anton Chekhov	£5.99
☐ TOP GIRLS	Caryl Churchill	£6.99
☐ A TASTE OF HONEY	Shelagh Delaney	£6.99
☐ STRIFE	John Galsworthy	£5.99
☐ ACROSS OKA	Robert Holman	£5.99
☐ A DOLL'S HOUSE	Henrik Ibsen	£5.99
☐ MY MOTHER SAID I NEVER SHOULD	Charlotte Keatley	£6.99
☐ DREAMS OF ANNE FRANK	Bernard Kops	£5.99
☐ BLOOD WEDDING	Federico Lorca	£5.99
☐ THE MALCONTENT	John Marston	£5.99
☐ BLOOD BROTHERS	Willy Russell	£6.99
☐ DEATH AND THE KING'S HORSEMAN	Wole Soyinka	£6.99
☐ THE PLAYBOY OF THE WESTERN		
WORLD	J.M. Synge	£5.99
☐ OUR COUNTRY'S GOOD	Timberlake Wertenbaker	£6.99
☐ THE IMPORTANCE OF BEING		
EARNEST	Oscar Wilde	£5.99
☐ A STREETCAR NAMED DESIRE	Tennessee Williams	£5.99

• All Methuen Drama books are available through mail order or from your local bookshop.

Please send cheque/eurocheque/postal order (sterling only) Access, Visa, Mastercard, Diners Card, Switch or Amex.

☐ ☐ ☐ ☐ ☐ ☐ ☐ ☐ ☐ ☐ ☐ ☐ ☐ ☐ ☐ ☐

Expiry Date: _____ Signature: _____

Please allow 75 pence per book for post and packing U.K.
Overseas customers please allow £1.00 per copy for post and packing.

ALL ORDERS TO:

Methuen Books, Books by Post, TBS Limited, The Book Service, Colchester Road, Frating Green, Colchester, Essex CO7 7DW.

NAME: _____

ADDRESS: _____

_____

_____

Please allow 28 days for delivery. Please tick box if you do not
wish to receive any additional information ☐

Prices and availability subject to change without notice.